W9-ADI-359

LOCAL GOVERNMENT IN-SERVICE TRAINING
an annotated bibliography

Edited by
Ronald M. Stout

WITHDRAWN
L. R. COLLEGE LIBRARY

sponsored by
Government Affairs Foundation, Inc.

GRADUATE SCHOOL OF PUBLIC AFFAIRS
STATE UNIVERSITY OF NEW YORK AT ALBANY
ALBANY, NEW YORK

CARL A. RUDISILL LIBRARY
LENOIR RHYNE COLLEGE

016.352
St 7L
62646
September, 1968

Government Affairs Foundation is a privately established, nonprofit, membership corporation of the State of New York, organized to advance and improve the science of government and the administration of public affairs.

The Foundation's principal activities include research, inquiries, studies, and the publication of reports and other works relating to the organization, powers, operations, and relationships of federal, state, and local governments, all in furtherance of the general and public welfare.

Copyright © 1968 by
Government Affairs Foundation, Inc.
Albany, New York

Library of Congress
Catalog Card Number: 67-65592

Printed in the United States of America
by the V-B Printing Company, Inc.
Albany, New York

Foreword

As stated by Mr. Justice Byron R. White in a recent decision of the United States Supreme Court *(Avery v. Midland),* "institutions of local government have always been a major aspect of our system, and their responsible and responsive operation is today of increasing importance to the quality of life of more and more of our citizens."

The services which local governments must provide today are varied and complex, particularly in our great urban centers. Administration of these programs and determination of local government policy as to scope and priority require greater knowledge and higher levels of proficiency than were needed in local government operations thirty, twenty, or even ten years ago.

Training of local officials and local government employees has almost unlimited potential for strengthening and improving the effectiveness of local governments in their efforts to respond adequately to these demands.

In 1965, Government Affairs Foundation initiated cooperation among several agencies, public and private, in a study of in-service training for local government officials and employees. As part of this study the Foundation undertook a preliminary survey of published materials which relate to in-service training of local government personnel or were applicable to that type of training.

This inquiry disclosed a wealth of valuable literature upon the subject and indicated the desirability of making the existence of these writings known to those seeking the expansion and improvement of such training programs as well as those endeavoring to strengthen our local governments generally and to increase the effectiveness of their operations.

For that purpose, the compilation of this annotated bibliography was sponsored by Government Affairs Foundation.

Dr. Ronald M. Stout, Professor of Political Science at the Graduate School of Public Affairs of the State University of New York at Albany, not only participated most helpfully as a member of the group which cooperated in the broad survey of in-service training initiated in 1965, but directed the compilation of and edited this bibliography. He coordinated with imagination, patient persistence and care the research performed in Berkeley, Chicago, New York, and Albany to produce a well integrated and useful reference work.

Professor Joseph F. Zimmerman, Director of the Local Government Studies Center of the Graduate School of Public Affairs of the State University of New York at Albany, was most helpful in advising on and handling the problems of publication. Rosalind B. Moore, as Project Planning Consultant of the Foundation, provided highly valuable services in the planning and preparation of this publication.

FRANK C. MOORE, President
Government Affairs Foundation

Albany, New York
April, 1968

Introduction

This bibliography, as indicated in the Foreword, orignated in a cooperative study of local government in-service training initiated by Government Affairs Foundation in 1965. An initial bibliography was developed on the basis of research in New York City and Albany. In New York City a search was made in the New York Public Library, its Municipal Reference Library, New York University Libraries, and other sources such as the Institute of Public Administration. In Albany, a search was made in the New York State Library, and specialized libraries of the New York State Office for Local Government, Training Section of the New York State Department of Civil Service, and Graduate School of Public Affairs of the State University of New York at Albany.

In the fall of 1966 it was decided by Government Affairs Foundation that a more comprehensive annotated bibliography on local government in-service training should be prepared and made available to those concerned with such training and with improvement of the public service in local governments in general. Arrangements were made to broaden the initial search for references to include the Library of the Institute of Governmental Studies of the University of California at Berkeley, and the Joint Reference Library plus the office collections of a number of national associations of governmental officials at 1313 East Sixtieth Street, Chicago, Illinois.

The search for references phase of the project was ended in May of 1967 although some items were added during the period when references were being annotated and editorial work was taking place. The search netted some 1300 items, and the final selection resulted in the inclusion of more than 900 references in the bibliography.

Several broad criteria of inclusion and exclusion guided the search for and final selection of references. One category of references constitutes the survey, description, or analysis of training needs, resources, and programs directly pertaining to local governments. Other broader categories included are books, articles, or reports which are general in nature, dealing with the purpose, development, organization, or evaluation of training programs, and with the techniques of training. However, these broader references were included subject to the requirement that they have potential application to local government training, or usefulness to those engaged in providing such training. This requirement foreclosed comprehensive coverage of the more general type of references since this would have been beyond the scope and purpose of the bibliography.

Two further requirements for selection were that the references should deal with in-service training and that the references be available in some published form in the libraries or organization offices in which bibliography research occurred. For example, no systematic effort was made to canvass state and local agencies for reports or monographs on training which had not reached the libraries in which the bibliographical search was conducted.

The bibliography, therefore, excludes references on pre-entry education or training, with a few exceptions. Omitted are articles or other references on graduate programs leading to a master's degree in public administration, even though these might be attended on a part-time basis by local government employees, as well as courses offered by colleges and universities through extension and adult education programs. The exceptions are internship programs and certain instances where courses were especially created for a particular group of local officials and not open to general attendance.

In addition, in the final selection of references for the bibliography, references on a particular function were not included if the number was too small to warrant classification as a separate function or as one of several interrelated functions which could be linked together under a common topical heading. Certain references were not included since they could not be located for annotation and did not seem vital enough to warrant listing without an annotation.

Although these criteria for selection of references are broad, it means that certain areas of local government functions are not represented in this bibliography, or at best are represented with relatively few references. For example, public education is staffed largely by persons whose preparation for their positions and subsequent improvement for on-the-job competence or upgrading is achieved primarily through programs in institutions of higher learning offering degrees for teachers and school administrators. For this and other reasons, public education is not included in the bibliography. As another example, it is known that certain large cities, such as New York City, have extensive training programs and activities. However, in the absence of articles, books, or monographs published in sufficiently formal form and distributed to libraries, the full range of such activities is not represented in this annotated bibliography.

The bibliography is divided into four major categories: Part I, Local Government Training in General; Part II, Training Generalist Officials and Administrators; Part III, Training Personnel in Functional Fields; and Part IV, Bibliographies. The categories and sub-categories of officials and employees, or types of functions appearing in the bibliography were derived inductively from the literature located during the search for references rather than being determined *a priori* in advance of the search. Further aspects of the organization of the bibliography, in relation to how the reader might make use of it, are covered in a subsequent section entitled "Guide to the Use of the Bibliography."

The contributions of others who worked on the development of this bibliography are too important and extensive to cover at this point and have been placed in a separate acknowledgments section to accord them the attention that they merit.

RONALD M. STOUT

April, 1968

Acknowledgments

The development and publication of this bibliography from its preliminary to final stages involved the work of a number of people. It is difficult to express adequately within the limits of available space the gratitude of the Editor and Government Affairs Foundation to each individual.

The Editor and the Foundation are particularly indebted to Miss Barbara J. Hudson, Librarian of the Institute of Governmental Studies of the University of California at Berkeley, to Miss Dorothy Simpson of the Institute's Library, and to the Institute. Upon being informed of the nature of the bibliography, Miss Hudson arranged for her participation and that of Miss Simpson in the compilation and annotation of references located in the Institute of Governmental Studies Library as part of the general service function of the Library since it was felt that the objectives and nature of the bibliography warranted this form of support. In addition to Miss Hudson and Miss Simpson providing a considerable number of annotated references to books, monographs, reports, and pamphlets, as well as citations to periodical articles for annotation in Albany and New York City, Miss Hudson was most helpful in suggesting a system to avoid overlap or duplication of annotation by the Institute of Governmental Studies Library and the Joint Reference Library in Chicago. She also advised on the extent to which various types of references located in the Institute's Library would be pertinent to the bibliography.

Mrs. Virginia Parker, Assistant Director of the Port Washington Library, Long Island, was of major assistance throughout the project. She compiled and annotated references using the New York Public Library, its Municipal Reference Library, New York University Libraries, and other sources such as the Institute of Public Administration and specialized libraries in New York City. She visited the Joint Reference Library in Chicago and recommended that this Library be consulted when it was decided to expand the bibliography for general publication. In addition to giving general advice on the development of the bibliography, Mrs. Parker also annotated references in periodicals compiled by the Institute of Governmental Studies Library and advanced the completion of the bibliography by helping in the initial editing of a number of the citations and annotations.

Mrs. Parker's original compilation was supplemented by references located by Mr. Roger P. Potocki and Miss Gail M. Keeton, Graduate Assistants in the Graduate School of Public Affairs of the State University of New York at Albany. Mr. Potocki compiled and annotated references in the New York State Library, specialized libraries of certain New York State government agencies, and the Library of the Graduate School of Public Affairs, while Miss Keeton annotated periodical references compiled by the Institute of Governmental Studies Library, re-reviewed references available in the New York State Library, and compared references gathered at all locations for possible duplications.

We are grateful to Mrs. Martha S. Gilchrist and to Mr. Joseph Benson— Librarians of the Joint Reference Library, 1313 East Sixtieth Street, Chicago, Illinois—for their initial and continuing assistance in arranging for the use of the resources of that Library and for their help in making arrangements for Miss Laverne Burchfield and Mrs. Jane S. Strable to work on this bibliography. This cooperation was provided since it was felt by Joint Reference Library that a bibliography on local government in-service training was needed. Also appreciated was the action of the International City Managers' Association in making available the bibliographic work which it had done on local government training as source material for the persons working on the bibliography in the Joint Reference Library.

We were fortunate that Miss Laverne Burchfield was willing to undertake an extensive search in the Joint Reference Library which produced a large number of references. Miss Burchfield at her own suggestion also reviewed the initial bibliography incident to her search in the Joint Reference Library, made corrections and suggestions for its improvement, and initiated a search in the office libraries of the various associations and organizations of officials at "1313". The cooperation of these associations and organizations of officials with Miss Burchfield, and later with

Mrs. Jane S. Strable, who also visited certain of these associations for additional reference items, was appreciated. The compilation of references was followed by Mrs. Strable's annotation of the references so compiled, a task involving several months of demanding work which she performed with an insistence upon thoroughness.

The Editor and the Foundation are indebted to Mrs. Hannah B. Applebaum, Bibliographer of the Graduate School of Public Affairs and author of several published bibliographies. Mrs. Applebaum brought her experience to bear in organizing and compiling the index, developing various ways in which it might be made more helpful to the user of the bibliography.

Several persons contributed to the improvement of the bibliography by reviewing it as a whole, or certain of its sections. Mrs. Rosalind B. Moore, Project Planning Consultant of the Government Affairs Foundation, reviewed the entire bibliography and made helpful suggestions on its content and organization. Mr. Hollis A. Swett, Director of Property Valuation of the Division of Equalization and Assessment, Mr. Anthony R. Granito, Supervisor of Fire Training of the Division of Fire Safety, and Mr. Orrell A. York, Executive Director of the Division of Municipal Police Training—all of the New York State Office for Local Government—reviewed the sections on Finance and Recording Officers, Fire Protection, and Police, respectively, and made suggestions for additions. Mr. Henry J. McFarland, Director of the Municipal Service Division of the New York State Department of Civil Service, made a critique of and gave advice on the overall organization and topical headings of the bibliography.

In addition, Mr. Richard A. Atkins, Deputy Commissioner of the Office for Local Government, gave advice on the categorization of references pertaining to planning, housing, and community development, and on what institutions, organizations, or kinds of persons might have an interest in the bibliography. His views were appreciated, as were those of Mr. Herbert M. Engel, Assistant Director of the Training Section of the New York State Department of Civil Service, who also advised on potential areas of interest in the bibliography for distribution purposes.

The process of publication, involving planning the format and style, preparation of manuscript, correction of citations, printing arrangements, and related aspects was coordinated by Professor Joseph F. Zimmerman, Director of the Local Government Studies Center of the Graduate School of Public Affairs. Professor Zimmerman also was a constant source of advice on the editing as well as being the coordinator for advancing the bibliography from manuscript to printed stage. Thanks are due to a number of graduate assistants working in the Local Government Studies Center for proofing and further checking in the library for details on citations under the supervision of Miss Mary E. Snyder, and special thanks are owing to Miss Betty Jones who typed and retyped initial and successive manuscripts, working after hours to complete this task as rapidly as possible. We also appreciate Mrs. Judith B. Lickona's technical assistance in developing the format to be followed by the printer and assistance in editing.

Liaison between the Editor and the Government Affairs Foundation office was provided by Miss Naomi Natcharian who, in addition to this assistance, also supervised the preparation of labels for a mailing list. Miss Mary A. Dobeck assisted in compiling the list to be used for distribution of the bibliography.

Finally, the Editor wishes to express his appreciation to the Government Affairs Foundation and its President, Mr. Frank C. Moore, and to Mrs. Moore, for their continuous interest in and constant support of the development of the bibliography, including their willingness to confer and give advice whenever necessary on various aspects of the bibliography.

RONALD M. STOUT

Guide To The Use Of The Bibliography

This bibliography consists of four major parts: Part I, Local Government Training in General; Part II, Training Generalist Officials and Administrators; Part III, Training Personnel in Functional Fields; and Part IV, Bibliographies.

The Table of Contents provides information in outline form on the scope and nature of the references covered within each major part through the topical headings and sub-headings under which the references are classified. The primary emphasis is on providing the user of the Bibliography with headings which will indicate the kind of training involved, either by function, or by the type of official, or both. For example, under Part III, Training Personnel in Functional Fields, the heading "Police" is subdivided into "General," "Cadet and Police Aide Programs," "Delinquency Control," "Minority Group Relations," "Riot Control," and "Traffic Control."

A secondary type of classification is employed if there are a sufficient number of references to justify a subordinate breakdown under the primary headings describing the kind of training or official. The secondary classifications or headings are used to indicate the kind or nature of the references involved; namely, (1) "Surveys, Descriptions, and Analyses of Local Training Needs, Resources, and Programs," (2) "General References on Purpose, Development, Organization, and Evaluation of Training Programs," and (3) "General References on Techniques of Training." The first kind of reference surveys, describes, or analyzes ongoing or past local training programs, or specific resources available to local units. The second kind of reference involves articles, monographs, or books which for the most part deal with the purposes of training or how one organizes or evaluates training programs in general. Even though the examples used in these general references are from national or state government or private enterprise, the references are included in view of their general applicability to training of local officials and employees. Thus a reference discussing executive development in general, with examples from the national government, might be helpful to a training officer planning an executive development program in a large city or metropolitan county. The third kind of reference is related to the second, but tends to focus on the specific skills, methodology, or devices for training. Although these references usually do not refer to local government, informative articles on the case method in training, the posting problems technique, or the use of audio-visual aids are as applicable to local government training as they are to national or state government training.

As with all classification systems, borderline cases develop. When a reference clearly is as much in one field as another, the reference is listed under both appropriate headings. In other instances, the editor has made an arbitrary choice by placing the reference under the heading or classification according to where the greatest emphasis or tendency seems to rest in the article or book. Finally, it should be stressed that the topical headings were developed inductively, so they do not have the orderliness of a system of headings determined *a priori*. On the other hand, they hopefully are more meaningful in terms of reflecting the actual focus of the references.

Part I of the Bibliography deals with books, monographs, or reports and articles pertaining to local government training without reference to any particular type of officer or functional field, or if types of employees or fields are involved, the reference covers such a composite of employees or fields as to resist classification under functional fields. The very generality of these references and the large number of them lead to using the three subordinate classifications referred to above. Those interested in knowing about the experiences of local governments in overall training programs, or how to organize and finance and evaluate training programs in general, or in discussions of techniques of training without reference to a particular functional field will find references along such lines in this Part.

Part II of the Bibliography pertains to a category of officials for which the descriptive headings are subject to considerable dispute, largely because of the difficulty of developing precise terminology. There are officials and administrators who are truly generalists, such as councilmen, members of boards of supervisors, mayors, and managers. There are also department heads, their deputies, and bureau, division, and section heads or supervisors who in varying degrees are functional officials but whose primary role is that of management and supervision. Again, although the intern is in a functional field, the concept of the internship is generalist in character, and may involve rotation from one field to another within a city government, or within a department, with the assumption that intern ultimately will become part of the managerial group.

Another differentiation between types of generalists is that of separating the elected representative or official who must run for office from the appointed manager or officer who may acquire his position by political appointment or by selection from a civil service list. Part II, then, organizes references under the three headings of "Elected Representatives and Executives," covering such officials as councilmen, members of boards of supervisors, mayors, town supervisors, and the like; "Appointed Managers, Executives, and Supervisors," dealing with a rather wide range of management personnel from city managers and department heads through bureau chiefs to section supervisors; and finally, "Interns and Trainees." Where appropriate, references also have been cross-listed under functional headings in the bibliography.

Part III of the bibliography covers the training of personnel in functional fields. In certain instances, such as "Corrections, Juvenile Delinquency, Probation, and Parole," the differentiation between types of personnel engaged in these closely interrelated functions was not sufficient in terms of the references available to warrant further functional subdivision. However, there was enough differentiation to warrant a secondary breakdown between surveys, descriptions, or analyses of local training needs, resources, and programs and general references on purpose, development organization and evaluation of training programs. In other instances, as in "Finance and Recording Officers," the references grouped readily into three functional subfields, namely "Assessors," "Finance Officers," and "County and Municipal Clerks," but not into the secondary classification of kinds of references. These varying situations prevailed in other fields, such as "Fire Protection" which broke down logically into secondary kinds of references, while "Health" subdivided more readily into sub-functional fields. Police, in which there was an unusually large number of references, provided both the primary breakdown of functional or type of official subfields, and the secondary subdivision kind of reference. Finally, the relatively small number of references located in some fields, such as "Libraries" or "Public Works" resulted in only the one major functional subheading being used, with all types of references lumped together alphabetically under the one major heading.

Part IV is largely self-explanatory, in that it consists of references on bibliographies on training, primarily of a general, functional, or type of official nature. These references were not cross listed under the functional headings, but listed solely under Part IV.

The index is organized primarily by author, or in the absence of an author, by issuing or publishing agency. In addition, the index refers to items according to major publishing agencies and major periodicals, and, where it seemed significant, key identifying elements of references as indicated in the annotations, such as names of places where training is taking place. To facilitate locating references from the index, a system is used whereby after the name of the author or publisher, the number of the page on which the reference may be found is indicated, followed by a lower case letter to show the sequential position of the item on the page. Thus, for example, an item in the index which reads Bray, F., 16c refers to the third item listed on page 16.

Contents

Part I
Local Government Training in General

A. Surveys, Descriptions, and Analyses of Local Training Needs, Resources, and Programs

Blitz, L. Franklin. "Municipal Employee Training," *Alabama Municipal Journal,* XXIV (June, 1966), 5-7.

A joint proposal of Auburn University and University of Alabama for training municipal employees as part of the first annual program for community services under the Higher Education Act of 1965. It describes briefly a comprehensive program for training department heads and for employee orientation training based on the Gadsden Comprehensive Training Program previously conducted by the Bureau of Public Administration of the University of Alabama. It also mentions other programs of the joint proposal and discusses limitations of training programs in general.

Bond, Philip J., and others. "Is In-Service Training a Worth-While Undertaking in Municipal Operations?," *Fourth Report on Conference on Municipal Administration.* Boston: Boston Administrative Services Department, November, 1959, 13-25.

This article comments on the reasons for training and the training programs for four occupations in the Boston government: the secretary, the social worker, the inspector, and the engineer.

Brennan, James J. "Improved Training and Information for Municipal Personnel," *Connecticut Government,* XV (June, 1962), 5-8.

Analysis of what has been done to provide training and informational aids needed by Connecticut's municipal employees. The author presents a general survey of needs and possible programs for Connecticut municipalities.

Brenneman, Leroy J. "New In-Service Training Program Graduates 466 Phoenix Employees," *Western City,* XXXII (August, 1956), 34.

A brief description is given of the in-service training program in Phoenix, Arizona and its achievements to date.

Bromage, Arthur W. "Ridley's Dream—In-Service Training," *Public Management,* XXXVIII (July, 1956), 150-52.

The entire July, 1956 issue of *Public Management* is a tribute to Clarence E. Ridley who retired as executive director of International City Managers' Association June 30, 1956. It is devoted to Ridley's success in spotlighting the need for in-service training and then providing the texts and programs to fulfill this need.

Brown, Milon. "Job Training on a Shoestring," *Public Personnel Review,* XXV (April, 1964), 119-23.

Describes how the city of Fort Lauderdale, Florida met the demands for an increase in personnel and higher job competence at all levels without a budgetary allocation for employee training or a qualified training man.

Brunton, Robert L. *Management Practices for Smaller Cities.* Chicago: International City Managers' Association, 1959, 430 pp.

Training needs are discussed on pages 144-152 with attention to the Beverly Hills, California program and the use of outside training facilities. The training of particular groups such as firemen and building inspectors is touched upon in other sections of the book.

Brunton, Robert L., and Schwab, Eleanor. "Municipal In-Service Training," *1960 Municipal Yearbook.* Chicago: International City Managers' Association, 1960, 251-60.

A summary of the results of a survey by the International City Managers' Association of the in-service training programs conducted in all cities in the United States with over 10,000 population. Among the topics covered are frequency of courses, organization for training, nature of training, organization of courses, and kinds of training available, with specific illustrations.

Buck, Thomas. "Chicago's Universities Blazing the Trail in Training Personnel for Urban Leadership: Professionalism Comes to Government," *Commerce,* LXII (July, 1965), 18-19.

The university centers for urban and metropolitan studies, their objectives and research, and the courses they offer are described in this article.

Cahill, William E. *Employee Training and Development Services.* Chicago: Chicago Civil Service Commission, February 8, 1966, v. p.

Contains a series of short descriptions of employee training and development services available to all city departments through the Chicago Civil Service Commission.

Conroy, Edward G. "In-Service Training at the Local Level," *Proceedings of the Eleventh Governor's Conference on State-Local Relations.* Amherst: Bureau of Government Research, University of Massachusetts, August 20-21, 1959, 27-30.

A description of the sources which are available to local officials in Massachusetts in the establishment of in-service training programs.

Corson, John J. "Better Personnel in Local Government," *Public Management,* XLIV (February, 1962), 34-36.

Presents preliminary findings of a study by the Municipal Manpower Commission.

Dinerman, Beatrice, and Dvorin, Eugene P. "Formal Education Programs for Local Government Employees," *Public Personnel Review,* XX (January, 1959), 33-38.

A survey of the educational opportunities offered by city and county jurisdictions throughout the country.

Directory of Training Programs in South Carolina for Municipal Officials and Employees. Columbia: Bureau of Public Administration, University of South Carolina, Annual.

A directory giving detailed descriptions of the programs and services sponsored by government agencies and designed primarily for municipal employees and officials. Some programs for county and state employees are included if they are open to municipal employees. This is an annual publication.

"Educational Incentive Plan Encourages Employee Training," *Western City,* XLI (March, 1965), 28, 30.

This article explains the implementation and effect of the adoption of the Educational Incentive Plan by Irivendale, California to encourage self-improvement in employees and to recognize and reward the individual employee for his accomplishments.

Esser, George H., Jr. "Basic Training Courses for Municipal Officials," *Popular Government,* XX (March, 1954), 10.

A brief and general overview of courses for training municipal officials offered by the Institute of Government of the University of North Carolina.

Furia, John J. *Training Municipal Employees New York City, 1940-41: A Review and a Forecast.* New York: Bureau of Training, New York City Civil Service Commission, 1941, 96 pp.

A history of the extensive training program, including the highlights of the first year. The content of one session each for two different courses, and charts of the training program and announcements of the courses also are presented.

Glassford, Albert F. "Inter-Community Cooperation Makes In-Service Training Possible: Fifteen Cities and Villages United to Provide Their Administrative Personnel With a Comprehensive Training Program on a Variety of Municipal Functions," *Michigan Municipal Review,* XXXIV (August, 1961), 217.

A general description of an in-service training program conducted by several cities and villages in Michigan including texts used, procedure in development of the program, and important by-products of the program.

Graves, W. Brooke. "An Intergovernmental Attack on Local Training Needs," *Personnel Administration,* XXII (May-June, 1959), 30-38.

The author discusses the present status of training—uneven quality, lack of coordination, and variety of organizational patterns—and suggests appropriate roles for local, state, and federal governments in attacking the problem.

————. *Public Service Training for Local Government in 1956: A Survey of Current Programs and Practices.* Washington, D.C.: Legislative Reference Service, United States Library of Congress, 1957, 256 pp.

Part I analyzes the historical background of local government training and the George-Dean Act of 1936, summarizes the findings of the survey, and suggests a program for the future. Part II covers the information received concerning training of local government personnel in forty-eight states, with respect to overall administration of such training, its financing, its actual operation, and the instructors involved in the training.

————. "Public Service Training for Local Government Personnel," *County Officer,* XXV (February, 1960), 54-56.

Describes the history of public service training for local government personnel with special emphasis on the effects of the George-Dean Act of 1936 and its revisions.

Guide on Tuition Reimbursement. Los Angeles: Los Angeles County Civil Service Commission, 1960, 36 pp.

On May 31, 1960, the Board of Supervisors adopted a tuition reimbursement program specifying policies, procedures, and conditions governing the reimbursement of employees for tuition for successfully completed courses related to their work. This guide was developed as an aid to departments to meet requirements for participation in the program.

Gunter, Elder. "City Employees Go To School: University City, Mo. Reports That Employee-Training Programs Help Reduce Costs and Increase Personnel Efficiency," *American City,* LXVIII (April, 1953), 106-07.

The city manager of a suburb of St. Louis reports on three types of training programs conducted by his city.

Hamlin, Clark, Baker, William, and McVean, James. *In-Service Training for County Officials.* Albany: County Officers Association, August, 1967, 172 pp.

Contains the report and findings of the In-Service Training Committee of the County Officers Association of New York State which had been appointed to investigate the feasibility of the Association expanding its services to include some form of in-service training. The Committee recommended "that the Constitution and By-Laws of the County Officers Association be amended in order to create a Standing Committee on In-Service Training," and "that the Association proceed to set up a program of In-Service Training for County Officials."

In-Service Training of Municipal Employees at Universities. Chicago: American Municipal Association, 1949, 19 pp.

Part One describes programs at universities in selected states and Part Two describes programs for selected kinds of personnel.

Ittner, Ruth. *Training Courses for Municipal Officials in Washington State.* Seattle: Association of Washington Cities, August, 1963, 6 pp.

"In-service training programs for municipal officials and employees have been developed by a number of organizations and agencies. . . . This bulletin lists the many courses available to city officials throughout the state and includes data in regard to persons eligible to enroll therein, the sponsors, when and where they are held, and the person to contact concerning them."

Klinger, T. S., and Lytgen, John. "Personnel Training in Savannah," *Georgia Local Government Journal,* II (May, 1952), 6-9.

The Savannah Civil Service Commission planned with the Savannah Vocational School to provide a program first for supervisory personnel, and then to encourage completion of high school and upgrade office skills. Police and fire training also are offered and have been made available to nearby communities. All training is to be on a voluntary basis.

Lathrop, Harold. *Orientation of Part-Time and Volunteer Personnel.* Lawrence: Governmental Research Center, University of Kansas, February 27, 1956, 21-24.

A brief statement of the problem of training volunteers is followed by comments and descriptions of specific programs.

Lee, Kendall H. "Meeting the Training Problem in Small Cities," *Mayor and Manager,* V (November, 1962), 20-21.

A description of some of the training devices used in Asbury Park, New Jersey to meet the problems of the severe strain put on municipal employees during the vacation season. The Asbury Park example could be applied to small cities having a limited budget and lacking staff capable of carrying out full scale training programs.

Let's Have a Look at the Training Picture in San Diego County. San Diego: Training Division, Department of Civil Service and Personnel, San Diego County, no date, 12 pp.

A brief discussion of training problems unique to the county service precedes suggestions for the kinds of training best offered in each department or on a county-wide basis. Services and programs of the Training Division are described.

Management Manpower Development. Sacramento: Committee on County Manpower Needs, County Supervisors Association of California, November, 1963, 14 pp.

Since considerations of time and money limit the availability of graduate and undergraduate study for county personnel, the Committee suggests as a solution for training problems the scheduling of short-term institutes and continuing courses given locally on a once or twice a week basis. The necessity for recruiting personnel of high quality is stressed and the results of a survey of reported recruiting difficulty of California counties is included.

Mason, Bruce B. "University Bureaus and Public Official Training," *Adult Education* (Spring, 1960), 166-70.

A commentary on the 1956 survey on public service training by W. Brooke Graves. The author notes that conferences usually do not exceed three days, trainees are in a sense self-selected, and that although individuals vary in abilities, perception, and interest, each expects to receive instruction in the specifics of his job. Typical programs become ninety per cent job training and ten per cent theory. It is recommended that more theory, standards of performance, and more written material be included in the programs and that bureau personnel in training be given a greater role in program planning and instructor selection.

Metropolitan Dade County Career Development Training Program: Formal Policy Statement. Miami: Dade County Department of Personnel, December, 1958, 29 pp.

A proposed plan providing for development and training of Dade County employees. The plan includes organizational framework, tools and resources, personnel development, assessing progress and evaluating results, and preliminary measures.

Miller, C. A. "On-the-Job Training Pays Dividends: An In-Service Training Program for All City Employees Has Resulted in Better Morale, Improved Public Relations, and More Effective Service to the Public," *Public Management,* XXXIV (August, 1952), 174-75.

A brief discussion of the in-service training program of Saginaw, Michigan, noting the different programs offered and the overall results of in-service training for this community.

Municipal Manpower Commission. *Governmental Manpower for Tomorrow's Cities.* New York: McGraw-Hill Book Company, Inc., 1962, 201 pp.

A study of the specialized personnel needs created by rapid urban growth, and the development of personnel systems necessary to attract and hold adequate numbers of competent people in managerial, technical, scientific, and other specialized positions. Although it deals only generally and briefly with the need for pre-entry and post-entry training for "ATP" personnel and the role of universities in filling the need, the report presents an overview of municipal manpower which is of importance to the person concerned with local government training.

3

Municipal Post-Entry Training Needs and Resources in California. Berkeley: League of California Cities, December, 1966, 62 pp.

This study is based on visits to forty cities and answers to detailed questionnaires returned from ninety cities in California. It "is intended to serve two basic purposes. First, for an overview of training needs among municipal employees. Second, it is expected to be helpful to faculty members at all institutions of higher education as a guide to training needs at the city level." Fairly detailed descriptions of the formal post-entry training policies of individual cities are included.

"Municipal Training Course Emphasizes How at University of North Carolina," *American City,* LI (December, 1959), 167.

A brief outline of the course offered to students of city government by the University of North Carolina's Institute of Government.

NALGO Correspondence Institute. London: National Association of Local Government Officers, 1945, 40 pp.

A description of the Institute and how it operates which also lists the courses offered for local government examinations.

Nolting, Orin F. *Post-Entry Training in the Public Service in Western Europe.* Chicago: International City Managers' Association, 1962, 106 pp.

A report showing how local governments in western Europe have developed post-entry training programs, the extent to which such training is provided, and how it is conducted. The study emphasizes programs for the training of administrative and executive personnel and also administrative training for professional and technical personnel who have administrative duties.

Olsen, Allan S. "Group Training for City Employees," *Public Management,* XXXV (August, 1953), 178-79.

An analysis is made of a brief survey of in-service training work in American cities conducted by the International City Managers' Association. The analysis notes the number of cities conducting programs, the areas in which training is given, and the procedures for implementing the program.

Perreault, John O. "Municipal Employees Go to School in Richmond: How a Municipal Training Program Conducted by the Public Schools Became the 'Talk of the Town,'" *Adult Leadership,* VII (October, 1958), 99-100.

A description of an experiment by Richmond, Virginia in using the public schools' adult education division as a municipal training department.

Post-Entry Training in the Local Public Service. Chicago: International City Managers' Association, 1963, 82 pp.

A report on post-entry training programs for administrative, professional, and technical personnel covering both on-the-job training and off-the-job training offered by local governments, educational institutions, institutes, and correspondence courses. Discussed are the need for training, in-service training being provided by local governments, training resources, guidelines for establishing programs, and problems in future prospects. Appendices include a list of training sources, a model statute and a model ordinance establishing training programs, and a selected bibliography.

Proceedings (of) Conference on Continuing Education for Public Administrators in State, County and City Government in California. Berkeley: Institute of Governmental Studies, University of California, 1965.

Held November 7-9, 1963, at the University of California at Davis, this "conference was called to identify the needs of state, county and city administrators for programs of continuing education, to ascertain the agencies most qualified to provide this education and to discuss the limitations and advantages of participation in such programs by institutions of higher learning." The Proceedings include the agenda of the four workshops, which were the core of the conference; the summary of workshop discussion and recommendations; conference speeches; and background papers.

Reining, Henry Jr., and Sherwood, Frank P. "25 Years of Education for the Public Service: One University's Experience," *Public Personnel Review,* XVI (October, 1955), 195-202.

The background, unique characteristics, some of the results of its operation, and the future expectations of the School of Public Administration at the University of Southern California are described in this article.

Reock, Ernest C., Jr. "In-Service Training Activities of the Rutgers Bureau of Government Research," *New Jersey Municipalities,* XXXIX (November, 1955), 20-23.

A statistical breakdown of the growth pattern, courses, and attendance for the first five years (1950-55) of the in-service training for employees of the municipalities, counties, and the state government conducted by the Rutgers University Bureau of Government Research.

Report on Present City of Milwaukee Employee Training Activities and Proposed New Programs for the 1967-68 Budget Period. Milwaukee: City Service Commission, 1966, 118 pp.

A report describing various categories of programs administered by the city, those administered by operating departments, and proposed programs. There is a recommended schedule for the development of the proposed programs and a budget. The Appendix includes a training questionnaire, relevant statistics, and samples of materials used in training programs.

Robinson, R. L. "Training Development in County Government," *County Officer,* XX (June, 1955), 138-40.

A brief discussion of reasons for the slow development of in-service training in county government and suggestions for starting a program.

Romani, John H. "Perspectives on Post-Entry Training for the Local Public Service," *Public Management,* XLV (July, 1963), 146-51.

A discussion of the need for post-entry training to meet the demands of the times, the status of local public service training programs in the United States, and suggestions for stimulating such training.

Schriever, Paul. "Municipal In-Service Training," *Public Management,* XLIV (August, 1962), 173-77.

An evaluation of municipal in-service training with emphasis on the current status of such training, training resources, what cities lack, what cities are doing to overcome problems in this area, and career personnel.

Stanley, David T. *Professional Personnel for the City of New York.* Washington, D.C.: The Brookings Institution, 1963, 461 pp.

Chapter eight of this book on New York City's personnel system deals with training and development, including the evaluation of a training program, the City's organizations and resources for training, in-service and outside training, executive and middle management development, the trainee programs, and city government training in general.

Stewart, Alva W. "Back to School for Tar Heel City Officials," *Public Management,* XLIX (February, 1967), 40-42.

Describes the work of the Institute of Government of the University of North Carolina and its municipal administration course which acquaints city officials with the "whole spectrum of municipal government."

Stoudemire, Robert H. *Directory of Training Programs in South Carolina for Municipal Officials and Employees.* Columbia: Bureau of Public Administration, University of South Carolina, 1962, 49 pp.

"The directory includes detailed descriptions of the programs and services designed primarily for municipal employees and officials and of those programs conducted for county and state employees which may be attended on occasion by municipal employees . . . grouped into sections according to the nature of the training provided."

Stover, Carl F. "To Improve the People Who Govern Our Cities," *Minnesota Municipalities,* LI (February, 1966), 34-36.

The Executive Director of the National Institute of Public Affairs, proposes ways to provide for a continuing supply of qualified personnel and for opportunities for continuing education in order to encourage excellence in local government service.

A Survey of In-Service Training Needs for California Local Governments. San Francisco: Griffenhagen-Kroeger, Incorporated, January, 1965, 37 pp.

A survey, with report and recommendations, conducted for the University of California Extension to assist it in preparing a state plan under Title VIII, Housing Act of 1964. It quotes extensively from the "Conference on Continuing Education for Public Administrators in State, County and City Government in California" and from material prepared for the Conference. The results of a questionnaire—"Local Government Training Needs"—sent to thirty-five cities and counties and one district are tabulated.

Training and Employee Relations. Honolulu: Training and Employee Relations Division, Honolulu Department of Civil Service, April, 1954, 10 pp.

A pamphlet which describes the organization and work of the Honolulu Training and Employee Relations Division, established in 1953. Included are reasons for establishing in-service training, topics covered by courses presented, and needs for additional in-service training.

University Scholarships for Experienced Municipal Career Administrators. Chicago: International City Managers' Association, 1963, 1 p.

This announcement contains information about the nature of the Career Education Awards, eligibility of participants, and how to apply for an award.

Westmeyer, Troy R. "The Boston Program for Government Employees—First Appraisal," *Personnel Administration,* XVII (July-August, 1954), 16-20.

A case history of the adult education program for government employees inaugurated at Boston University in February, 1953.

"Why Train? Pre-Entry and Post-Entry Training Programs for City Employees Plus Guides for Starting Your Own Local Training Program," *Public Management,* XLIX (February, 1967), 33-42, 48-49.

Pertinent articles in this special issue include an editorial on the need for training; guidelines for planning, developing, and administering a program; a description of the University of North Carolina program for managerial personnel of cities; and a work-study intern program conducted by the University of Notre Dame and Buchanan, Michigan.

"Wide Range of Training Offered to Government Officials and Employees," *Internal Affairs,* XXVII (March, 1962), 20-24.

This article reports on the courses offered by major Pennsylvania colleges and universities, and the State Department of Public Instruction.

Zaner, Theodore. "Programmed Instruction and Its Use in the Public Service," *Public Personnel Review,* XXVII (April, 1966), 133-35.

The author presents the results of a survey of twenty-five public service activities in the New York City area which indicated that very little use is being made of programmed instruction.

B. General References on Purpose, Development, Organization, and Evaluation of Training Programs

"Assessing the Value of Training," *Public Personnel Review,* XX (January, 1959), 66-70.

This article is a description of the current state of the training art. It contains suggestions for making research an integral part of training programs.

Automatic Data Processing: Digest of Selected Seminar Presentations. Washington, D.C.: United States Civil Service Commission, 1962, 127 pp.

Programs were conducted to acquaint government employees at middle and top levels of management with the various considerations involved in automatic data processing (ADP), and in so doing, improve the management of ADP.

Brown, David S. "An Old Tool Holds New Promise for Management," *Public Management,* XLVII (November, 1965), 288-91.

An argument is made for the as yet untapped "true potential" of training. The author attempts to indicate what this potential is through a series of examples chosen to show what training really is and what it can do.

Brunton, Robert L. *A Manual for Municipal In-Service Training.* Chicago: International City Managers' Association, 1960, 40 pp.

Aimed at the "chief administrator who must plan, administer and evaluate training programs," this manual discusses: the importance of training; problems of organizing a training program; in-service training methods; the conference method and its variations; and how to evaluate and make training more effective. There is an additional section on visual aids.

Caldwell, Lynton K. "Determining Training Needs for Organizational Effectiveness," *Personnel Administration,* XXVI (March-April, 1963), 11-19.

Effective training programs require a tie-in with the general policies and programs of the organization. Specific needs can best be determined by manpower surveys; realistic cost data should also be ascertained.

————. "Measuring and Evaluating Personnel Training," *Public Personnel Review,* XXV (April, 1964), 97-102.

This is a discussion of the principles and criteria of measurement and evaluation of personnel training in an attempt to dispel the belief that the impact of training is too complex to be measured and that the variables involved are too great to permit fair evaluation.

————. "University Assistance in Training Public Personnel," *Public Personnel Review,* XIV (October 1953), 151-60.

This is a discussion of the necessity for, as well as mutual advantage of, cooperative programs between universities and government agencies, outlining just what universities do for these programs and the need which they will fill for training personnel for government service.

Carrell, Jeptha J. "An Appraisal of Municipal In-Service Training," *Public Management,* XL (October, 1958), 237-41.

An eleven-step procedure is presented for setting up an in-service training program. Some training programs, texts, and instructional material, many of which are available from the International City Managers' Association, are described.

Effective Use of Supplementary Resources in a Staff Development Program. Washington, D.C.: Division of Technical Training, Bureau of Public Assistance, United States Social Security Board, 1942, 14 pp.

Describes ways in which institutes, lectures, study groups, committees, and conferences may be effectively used for the benefit of both agency and workers.

"Employee Training," *Municipal Personnel Administration.* Chicago: International City Managers' Association, 1960, 110-40.

This chapter deals with pre-entry and in-service training, training courses, methods, and administrative policies of municipal employee training. Definitions, evaluations, suggestions, and speculations concerning aspects of employee training are offered.

Engelbert, Ernest A. "Major Issues in Professional Training for Public Administration," *International Review of Administrative Sciences,* XXX (1964), 272-86.

Stating that any resolution of different views with respect to issues and aspects of professional training programs narrows down to the question what are we training for, the author feels that the issues may be identified under four principal categories: educational philosophy, concepts of the public service, content of training programs, and student qualifications.

Ewing, Russell H., and Ewing, Nadine R. "Training and Development Policies: A Review of the Need and the Factors to Consider," *Training Directors Journal,* XIX (June, 1965), 28-30.

This article discusses the formulation and classification of training and development policies.

Gardner, Neely D. "Training As a Framework for Action," *Public Personnel Review,* XVIII (January, 1957), 39-44.

"The function of training as we see it is to set up a communications network for management and for the worker. Within this communications network are provided mechanics for exploration of any kind of organization problem."

Graves, W. Brooke. "Education and Training for the Public Service," *Public Administration in a Democratic Society.* Boston: D. C. Heath and Company, 1950, 150-72.

The varieties of training—pre- and post-entry education and training, job instruction, and off-the-job training, are discussed. Planning training programs, putting them into operation, and methods to be used are covered briefly.

Hacon, R. J. *Conflict and Human Relations Training.* New York: Pergamon Press, 1965, 118 pp.

This book covers the nature of the problem, some remedies and approaches, and case histories.

King, S. D. M. "Automation and the Evaluation of Training," *International Labor Review,* XCII (September, 1964), 209-25.

The author outlines the new types of skills demanded by automated processes, and discusses various criteria that can be used for evaluating training programs and techniques.

Kirkpatrick, Donald L., and others. "Should the Training Function Be Located Within the Personnel Office, or Should It Report Directly to Management?," *Personnel Administration,* XXIV (July-August, 1961), 57-60.

Five different writers respond to the title question and each offers an individualized viewpoint.

Maguire, DeWitt. *Essential Elements of an Effective Over-All Training Program in Governmental Jurisdictions.* Detroit: Detroit Civil Service Commission, 1952, 14 pp.

The author discusses nine factors to be considered in setting up a coordinated training program—awareness of management responsibility, sound training philosophy, continuous determination of needs, participation on all levels, determination of content, selection of methods, adequate training facilities, coordination of effort, and follow-up evaluation.

McKnight, H. P., and others. "What Are the Considerations for Administering the Training Program Independently of the Personnel Program?" *Personnel Administration,* XXIX (September-October, 1966), 13-16; and (November-December, 1966), 27-30.

Training officers present reasons for independent administration of training programs.

"Municipal Work Simplification," *Management Information Service* (April, 1954), entire issue.

A definition of municipal work simplification, some of the functions to which it can be applied, basic principles, and methods.

Nigro, Felix. "The Role of In-Service Training," and "The Training Program in Action," *Public Personnel Administration.* New York: Henry Holt and Company, 1959, 226-93.

Two chapters in this book deal with the necessity and techniques of in-service training, including a discussion of purposes, definitions, evaluations, and models.

Oakes, James W. "The Administrative Aspects of Training," *Mayor and Manager,* V (November, 1962), 14-15.

An argument for the importance of training and suggestions for the basic requirements of any training program.

Price, Kendall O. "Training: An Intersection of Professions," *Personnel Administration,* XXIX (September-October, 1966), 45-48.

The responsibilities of the training director with respect to the various components of a training program are presented in some detail.

Rosenberger, Homer T. *How to Organize and Administer an Employee Training Program.* Washington, D.C.: Society for Personnel Administration, April, 1956, 35 pp.

"This manual has been prepared for the use of line executives and training directors in business corporations and government agencies having approximately 1,000 or more employees. It discusses some goals that are basic in the developing of a large staff by means of training. It attempts to assist executives and training directors to anticipate problems which occur frequently in the planning and conducting of employee training, and thus reduce the number and complexity of these problems."

Schlesinger, Lawrence. "Evaluating the Content of Multiple-Skill Training Programs," *Personnel Administration,* XXI (July-August, 1958), 20-27, 34.

Three methods of evaluating the contribution of a multiple-skill training course to the skills and knowledge required for job performance are described, the results are illustrated, and the limitations of the methodology are discussed.

Schrader, George R. "In-Service Training—Challenge for City Administration," *Texas Town and City,* LI (October, 1964), 17-19.

The author provides a systematic method of developing a training program which includes discovering needs, cultivating a conducive climate, and inventorying, marshaling, and utilizing resources.

Seckler-Hudson, Catheryn. "Appropriate Training and Development," *Organization and Management: Theory and Practice.* Washington, D.C.: Department of Government and Public Administration, American University, 1955, 169-74.

A point-by-point discussion of what training programs should do, followed by reasons for lack of progress in this field.

Shaw, Kennedy. "Municipal Employee Training: A Small Investment That Pays Large Dividends," *Mayor and Manager,* III (November, 1960), 6-8.

This article discusses the types of training which can be undertaken practicably, sources that can be turned to for training programs, and results that can be expected.

Smith, Norman R., Kopec, Chester J., Brown, Milon, and Claros, Thomas S. *Getting the Most for Your Training Dollar.* Chicago: Public Personnel Association, 1966, 22 pp.

Demonstrates how public agencies can give systematic attention to training with little or no expenditure of additional funds. Provides a list of helpful tips for operating a low-cost training program, and case histories of successful training programs conducted on limited budgets.

"Staff Training—It Takes New Techniques to Get Good Results," *Journal of Housing,* X (August-September, 1953), 272-73.

This article summarizes and quotes from an article by Charles S. Weber of the Michigan Civil Service Commission entitled "Getting Results from Training," in the May, 1953 issue of *State Government.* It includes a list of what Mr. Weber considers the fundamentals in setting up an employee training program.

Stahl, O. Glenn. "Staff Development and Training," *Public Personnel Administration.* New York: Harper and Bros., 1956, 335-80.

Chapter fifteen of this book deals with pre-entry training, in-service training, development of training policy, training needs, and forms and methods of training. It outlines various steps in a systematic approach to the problem of training.

To Help You Do Your Own Training. Lansing: Michigan Civil Service Commission, 1959, 29 pp.

Consists of lists having to do with job training, skills, functions, principles, needs, programs, kinds of presentation techniques, and visual aids.

"Training for the Municipal Service," *The Techniques of Municipal Administration.* Chicago: International City Managers' Association, 1958, 191-214.

This chapter was designed to aid the administrator in finding the answers to what should be taught, how instruction should take place, and who should be trained.

"The Training Function Budget," *Journal of the American Society of Training Directors,* XIII (November, 1959), 36-44, 46-48.

Report No. 5 of a study of the status and functions of training departments is concerned with what it costs, or should cost, to support the training function of an organization.

Training in the Public Service of Canada: A Report for the Fiscal Years 1947-48 and 1948-49. Ottawa, Canada: Staff Training Division, Civil Service Commission, 1950, 26 pp.

Describes training programs implemented during the two years. It is divided according to training methods and whether the course was departmental, central, service-wide, or external.

Training in the Public Service of Canada, A Supplementary Report, April 1949 to December 1950. Ottawa, Canada: Staff Training Division, Civil Service Commission, 1951, 34 pp.

This report, which describes various Canadian training programs implemented during this period, is divided according to methods used and whether the program was departmental, central, service-wide, or external.

Willis, Charles A. "City Training Nears Point of No Return," *Public Management*, XLIX (February, 1967), 35-39.

The Director of Training of Chicago's Civil Service Commission presents a set of guidelines for planning, developing, and administering municipal training programs in large and small cities.

C. General References on Techniques of Training

Broadwell, Martin A. "Training the Trainers," *Personnel*, XLVIII (September-October, 1966), 50-55.

Reasons are given for mediocrity in instruction, how to upgrade it and classroom techniques, and how to develop proper concepts of learning.

The Case Method: A Technique of Management Development. Washington, D.C.: Society for Personnel Administration, 1957, 32 pp.

This publication contains the proceedings of an all-day workshop on case study methods. The contents include philosophy and objectives, qualities and construction, and climate and participation and how they change people. Also given are notes on the seminar discussions, questions from the conferees, bibliography, and an evaluation questionnaire.

Gardner, Neely D. "Training," *Personnel Report No. 654.* Chicago: Public Personnel Association, 1965, 30-44.

A general discussion briefly touching on learning theory, putting theory into practice, and some training methods. It includes "A Checklist for Trainers."

Guetzkow, Harold. *Training for Policy Making Roles Through Organizational Simulation.* Evanston: Department of Political Science, Northwestern University, 1958, 4 pp.

A description of the new technique of role playing in an "organizational simulation"—defined as any "man-computer system contrived for the purpose of representing in reduced form the essential characteristics of an organization."

Guides for Instructional Management and Selected Training Techniques. Washington, D.C.: Office of Employee Development, Division of Management, United States Social Security Administration, 1963, 37 pp.

This pamphlet is designed as a self-study unit for trainers. It covers a course development guide, the seminar method, the workshop method, lesson planning, instruction critique, student exercises, and reading assignment.

Hints to Good Instruction. Washington, D.C.: Office of Employee Development, Division of Management, United States Social Security Administration, 1963, 25 pp.

An outline of instructional management and classroom administration. The major headings are: Stages of Instruction; Classroom Checklist, Classroom Management, and Training Aids.

Hookey, Edward M. *Guide to the Preparation of Training Materials.* Washington, D.C.: United States Bu-

reau of Employment Security, 1961, 75 pp.

A study explaining the primary factors involved in the preparation of training materials and showing method and techniques used in writing each of the three major types of instructional units.

Klein, Charles T., and Engel, Herbert M. "Programmed Learning and the Government Service," *Public Personnel Review*, XXIII (October, 1962), 223-26.

A brief discussion of the advantages, disadvantages, and basic precepts regarding teaching machines and programmed texts.

Michigan Civil Service Commission. Training Division. *A Guide to Training Practices.* Chicago: Public Personnel Association, 1966.

A guide in the form of simple lists of what to do, what not to do, who should do what, and descriptions of visual aids.

Sulkin, Howard A. *The Case Method.* Chicago: Industrial Relations Center, University of Chicago, 1966, 12 pp.

This discussion of the case method includes kinds of cases, advantages and disadvantages, role of the leader and his problems, criteria for a good case, how to write a case, and how to evaluate achievements.

Solem, Allen R. "Human Relations Training: Comparison of Case Study and Role Playing," *Personnel Administration*, XXX (September-October, 1960), 29-37.

This article examines ways in which role playing and case study appear to be alike, scrutinizes some comparative experimental data, and tries to arrive at meaningful distinctions between the two methods.

Teaching Methods and Techniques. Washington, D.C.: Office of Employee Development, Division of Management, United States Social Security Administration, 1962, 17 pp.

A pamphlet consisting of brief descriptions of the various methods of presenting material—lecture, conference, and case study—with the advantages and disadvantages listed for each.

Training Methods and Techniques. Washington, D.C.: United States Civil Service Commission, January, 1966, 53 pp.

Specific subjects covered are case method, coaching, incident process, in-basket exercise, job rotation, management games, role playing, sensitivity training, team training, and selecting and using visual aids.

Weaver, Fred D. "Use of T-Groups in the Public Service," *Public Personnel Review,* XXVII (October, 1966).

A report of the author's experience with a series of eight T-groups involving sixty-four people sponsored by the personnel office of Oakland, California. Quotations from participants in the groups are featured.

Whitesell, William E., and Pietrus, Joseph T. "Training and the Learning Process," *Personnel,* XLVII (July-August, 1965), 45-50.

This article summarizes the prerequisites of an effective training program and identifies the principal steps involved in learning.

Part II
Training Generalist Officials and Administrators

A. Elected Representatives and Executives

"Commissioners Enthusiastic About Georgia County Workshop," *Better Roads,* LII (February, 1962), 15-17.

A description of the content of two sessions—organization of the State Highway Department, and Planning, Constructing, and Maintaining County Roads—of the experimental workshop established to provide general information for county commissioners relating to their duties in local government.

"Dateline Indianola: The League's First School," *Iowa Municipalities,* XVII (February, 1962), 12, 25.

The first short-course school for municipal officials sponsored by the League of Iowa Municipalities and the Institute of Public Affairs of the State University of Iowa consisted of a general session and separate sessions for mayors, councilmen, and clerks.

"Dateline Spencer: The League's Second School," *Iowa Municipalities,* XVII (February, 1962), 14.

This article contains a brief, general description and the complete program for the one-day school held in conjunction with the regular monthly meeting of the Northwest Iowa Mayors' Association.

Gardner, Howard. "Orientation Programs for New Mayors and Councilmen," *Public Management,* XLI (1959), 158-61.

The author contends that although orientation conferences for newly elected municipal officials are held in many states, they generally meet with a notable lack of interest on the part of those eligible to attend despite an estimate that 99 out of every 100 come to their responsibilities with little, if any, background of experience likely to be helpful in the municipal decision-making function.

Howard, S. Kenneth, ed. *Proceedings of the Moderators' Workshop.* Durham: Public Administration Service, Department of Government, University of New Hampshire, 1965, 44 pp.

This workshop marked the first time in New Hampshire history that Moderators of towns and city wards throughout the state met as a group. The proceedings include three major speeches, the material discussed during the question periods of each, and summaries of six simultaneous discussion groups.

Mayor & Councilmen's Institute . . . Annual Conference. Phoenix: League of Arizona Cities & Towns, Annual.

Topics of timely interest and general application are presented to elected municipal officials at the Institute held in conjunction with the Annual Conference of the League. Also included is the President's Annual Report. The Institute was originally intended as training for newly-elected officials, but a separate one-day institute for that purpose was established in 1965.

Municipal Policy and Program Goals, An Advanced Course for Councilmen, Commissioners, and Supervisors, November 9, December 14, 1960. Pittsburgh: Institute of Local Government, University of Pittsburgh, 1960, 37 pp.

A training manual for a course designed to give councilmen, commissioners, and supervisors "an opportunity to review and evaluate their work as municipal legislators." The manual includes course outlines, discussion questions, and other data.

Municipal Problems. Albany: Conference of Mayors and Other Municipal Officials of the State of New York, Annual.

The Proceedings of the annual meeting of the Conference of Mayors and Other Municipal Officials of the State of New York between 1910 and 1958. In 1934, the name of the Proceedings was changed from *City Problems* to *Municipal Problems.*

The Office of Town Supervisor. Albany: The Association of Towns of the State of New York, 1960, 94 pp.

Prepared by the staff of the Association as part of its program of education and in-service training of town officers, this manual discusses the powers and duties of town supervisors.

Proceedings of the Institute for County Commissioners. Olympia: Washington (State) Association of County Commissioners, 1965.

These proceedings include addresses by government officials and staff of the Division of Governmental Studies and Services of Washington State University. The purpose of the Institute was to provide a thorough, systematic orientation for newly-elected commissioners together with a refresher for incumbents.

Proceedings of the Institute for Mayors, Councilmen, and Commissioners. Austin: Texas Municipal League, 1964.

An institute for elected officials which offered basic review of their powers, functions, duties, and responsibilities, and also offered studies in depth of prominent current interest areas.

Proceedings of the Mayors' and Councilmen's Institute. . . . Berkeley: League of California Cities, Biennial.

This biennial institute serves as a refresher for experienced officials and an orientation for newly elected officials. It is organized to give a comprehensive view of their duties and responsibilities.

Proceedings of the School for County Commissioners: A Collection of Addresses Presented at the Training School for County Commissioners and Chief Clerks. Harrisburg: Department of Internal Affairs, State of Pennsylvania, 1964, 62 pp.

This school was held to "acquaint new commissioners with the nature of their duties and to disseminate new information to those who previously held office."

Proceedings of the . . . Vermont Town Officers' Educational Conferences. Burlington: Government Research Center, University of Vermont, 1966.

A digest of the proceedings of the one-day sessions held in different locations in Vermont. Attendees "learn about what other towns are doing" and "get information for improving own work."

1959 School for Newly Elected County Commissioners in North Carolina. Chapel Hill: Institute of Government, University of North Carolina, April, 1959, 275 pp.

A summary of the instruction and discussion by members of the Institute staff covering most aspects of county government.

The Town Board. Albany: The Association of Towns of the State of New York, 1962, 107 pp.

This training manual was prepared by the staff of the Association as part of its program for the education of town officers. The manual covers classes of town, authority of the town board, town board meetings, fiscal matters, ordinances, town officers and employees, special districts, fire protection, and municipal cooperation.

The Urban Affairs Program, 1967. Washington, D.C.: National Institute of Public Affairs, no date, 8 pp.

A description of the first major activity of the Program which consisted of conferences on "The Metropolitan Area, Its Prospects and Problems," plus brief information on other urban affairs activities, designed for political, governmental, and community leaders.

Zimmerman, Joseph F. "Clark University Holds Seminar for Selectmen," *National Municipal Review,* XLVIII (January, 1959), 24.

Describes the first seminar of its kind for Massachusetts selectmen designed to give them help with specific problems and provide a broader orientation and outlook on local governmental problems.

B. Appointed Managers, Executives, and Supervisors

1. Surveys, Descriptions, and Analyses of Local Training Needs, Resources, and Programs

Administrative Trainee Program. Los Angeles: Chief Administrative Officer, Los Angeles County, September 18, 1963, 6 pp.

This report covers in some detail the recruiting, appointment, training, evaluation, and placement procedures of the county system and lists initial department assignments of trainees for a ten-year period.

Alves, Euro, and Hardy, William R. "Evaluating Supervisory Training in Los Angeles County," *Training Directors Journal,* XVII (August, 1963), 36-40.

The authors outline specific objectives of the evaluation, describe the research based on two questionnaires, give some of the results of the latter, and make recommendations.

Bollens, John C. "Municipal Management Training—An Appraisal," *Public Management,* XXXII (July, 1950), 146-49.

This is a summary and evaluation, after fifteen years, of the unique program of the International City Managers' Association's Institute for Training in Municipal Administration.

City Managers Training School. Lawrence: Governmental Research Center, University of Kansas, Annual.

Summaries of many of the presentations and group discussions. In recent years (the school was first held in 1950), a general theme has been selected and attention given to broader problems of public management rather than to the specific, routine, operational problems.

Cloner, Alexander. "Workshop for City Managers," *Public Management,* XLIV (August, 1962), 183.

A description of a conference of fifty city managers and their assistants at the University of Southern California, which was held as part of a program of continuing education and training sponsored by the University's School of Public Administration.

"Counties Plan Administrative Training Foundation," *Public Management,* XLV (August, 1963), 184-85.

This article gives a brief description of the purpose for the training foundation, sponsored by the County Supervisors Association of California and private industry. It cites reasons why county administrators are needed.

Department Managers Development Conference. Minneapolis: International City Managers' Association, Twin Cities Chapter, 1958.

An outline of the eight conference lectures written by the conference participants. The subjects covered were the manager's job, organization and work planning, relationships with others, public relations, supervision, and motivation.

"Development of Management Personnel," *Public Management,* XXXVII (February, 1955), 29-36.

A report, prepared for discussion at the fortieth annual conference of the International City Managers' Association held at St. Petersburg, Florida, December 5-8, 1954, which points out that business and industry have outstripped local government in the development of management personnel. The areas where public management is likely to be weak are discussed, and methods of improvement are proposed.

Ecklund, Lowell. "Training in Municipal Supervision," *Michigan Municipal Review,* XXXVI (May, 1964), 119.

The author describes the educational program in municipal supervision of the Office of Continuing Education, Oakland University from the first courses in 1958 through the expansion of geographical enrollment to off-campus courses in Macomb County.

Effective Supervisory Practices. Chicago: International City Managers' Association, 1965.

This series of bulletins is used for in-service training of supervisory personnel employed by cities, counties, and other local governments.

Elementary Supervision. Miami: Dade County Personnel Department, no date, 27 pp.

An outline of a course presented by Dade County, intended for the use of participants taking the course.

Elliott, Clarence H. "Training Supervisors in Human Relations," *Public Management,* XXXI (July, 1949), 194-96.

A program for foremen and supervisors in Jackson, Michigan which used the conference method, a leader's manual prepared by the city personnel department, and various films from the United States Office of Education.

The Executive Program for the City of New York and Metropolitan Area. New York: Graduate School of Public Administration and Social Service, New York University, 1960.

The need, the purpose, the organization, and the curriculum of the program are described.

Finklestein, Samuel B. "Newark Offers Executive Training for Top-Level Personnel," *New Jersey Municipalities,* XXXVIII (June, 1961), 12-16.

A description of Newark's beginning activities in training

programs for executives, the intergovernmental cooperation involved, and the steps taken in a specific program.

First Annual Short Course for Managers: Advanced Management Training Program, Chicago, Illinois, May 1-7, 1960. Chicago: International City Managers' Association and the University of Chicago, 1960, 3 pp.

This course gives general information about the course, the subjects to be offered, and the faculty.

Fourteenth Annual Short Course for Florida City Managers, April 24-27, 1960, . . . A Summary Record of the Proceedings. Tallahassee: Florida City Managers' Association, 1960, 15 pp.

The addresses and the panel discussions of the proceedings are summarized.

Hardy, William R. "An Executive Development Program—A Preliminary Report; Program Outline for County of Los Angeles," *Training Directors Journal,* XIX (March, 1965), 35-41.

Article includes reasons for failures in other similar programs, the training program principles established by the County, the suggested plan for structuring of departmental training programs, and hopes for the future of the plan.

Hardy, William R., and others. "What Lessons Have Been Learned About Supervisory Training in the Last Few Years?" *Personnel Administration,* XXVII (May-June, 1964), p. 47-49, 51.

Presented are brief opinions of four experts bearing on the question.

Harrell, C. A., and Heisel, W. D. "Developing City Employees," *Public Management,* XLIV (August, 1962), 178-81.

Reports a specific example (in Cincinnati) of the formulation of a training policy and describes briefly the training effort currently being expended in supervisory development.

Hinds, George L. *A Review of Executive Development Programs at Wayne State University, 1953-1961.* Detroit: Government Research and Service Staff, Department of Political Science, Wayne State University, July 30, 1961, 16 pp.

Programs presented for federal, state, and local executives are described, with lists of instructors and participants. A discussion entitled "A Statement of Philosophy; Executive Development for Public Executives" by Nathan D. Grundstein based on experience with the program, is included.

Hobart, James C. "Seminars for Administrative Assistants," *Public Management,* XLVI (May, 1964), 114.

The role of seminar training in the decentralization of administrative organization in Tucson, Arizona is discussed in this article.

Hollinger, Lindon S. "Los Angeles County Administrative Training Program," *County Officer,* XXIII (June, 1958), 112-13.

Initiated in 1933, the Los Angeles county administrative

training program now boasts many outstanding graduates with fifty-three former trainees currently employed in Los Angeles county.

"In-Service Training for Department Heads Gets Results in Dallas," *Public Management,* XXVII (October-November, 1945), 309-11.

A description of the development of the program, how it was conducted, and its results. The International City Managers' Association course in Municipal Administration was used.

Lucas, Norman A. "Are You Ignoring Your Most Valuable Assets?: Recruited with Great Care, Department Heads Often Are Not Encouraged to Further Their Job Abilities," *Mayor and Manager,* IX (May, 1966), 28-29.

This article deals with the program developed in New Canaan, Connecticut to prevent lethargy from creeping into the departments of municipal government. Started in 1962, the program is conducted in seminars which emphasize the problems and functions of each office.

Mailick, Sidney. *The Executive Program for the City of New York and Metropolitan Area.* New York: Graduate School of Public Administration, New York University, June, 1964, 38 pp.

The program described in this publication is intended to fill a need for the education and development of higher civil servants in the New York metropolitan area. It is an integral phase of the New York City Department of Personnel program. Methods employed are conferences, lectures, and workshops.

McNeill, Robert J. *A Study of the Feasibility of Mid-Career Education for Local Government Employees in the Detroit Metropolitan Area.* Detroit: Metropolitan Fund, 1966, 67 pp.

A "study which seeks to identify the conditions under which an effective mid-career education program could be established in the Detroit metropolitan area." It seeks to answer such questions as the recognition of the need for such education; the legal authority to participate; means of financing; patterns of participation; full-time residence, part-time residence; length and timing of a program; program content; credit or non-credit; undergraduate or graduate; number of participants; and procedure for selecting participants.

Moore, Paul. "How the City of Saginaw Trains Its Supervisors," *Michigan Municipal Review,* XXV (September, 1952), 152-53, 158.

The efforts of the City of Saginaw, Michigan, and Michigan State College to find ways of making city government operate more effectively are discussed. The article outlines the point of view of the college, setting up the program, problems such as the relationship to workers and improving teamwork, and an evaluation of the program.

Morris, Theodore P. "Cut the Cloth to Fit the Supervisor," *Public Personnel Review,* XVIII (July, 1957), 144-50.

A report on the management and supervisory training program of the city of Pasadena.

Municipal Administrative Management In-Service Education and Training. Berkeley: League of California Cities, September, 1963, 12 pp.

"The purpose of this paper is to outline what is believed are the training needs of personnel in the field of administrative management in California cities. It is intended to reflect the position of municipal administrators, including city managers, department heads and, to some extent, middle management personnel, in terms of educational needs which are most likely to be satisfied through association with academic institutions."

"Municipal Administrative Management In-Service Education and Training," *Conference on Continuing Education for Public Administrators.* Berkeley: Institute of Governmental Studies, University of California, 1965, 85-91.

This is one background paper prepared by the League of California Cities for the Proceedings of a Conference on Continuing Education for Public Administrators in State, County, and City Government in California. (See annotation of the Proceedings below). The paper covers educational and training needs, both broadly theoretical and professionally specific. Educational methods and problems of participation and finance are included.

Municipal Administrator Educational-Development Program: A Proposal to Meet the Needs of California Cities for Continuing Education and Development of Their Management Personnel. Berkeley: Institute for Local Self Government, January 3, 1964, 8 pp.

The basic assumption of this report is that post-entry educational needs at the management level can best be satisfied by academic institutions. The proposal is that a consultant be hired to identify, analyze, and evaluate needs for and current availability of academic resources and to identify conditions which limit use of existing resources. The resulting reports and recommendations would be discussed in a series of meetings with local government personnel. An estimated budget for the project is included.

Nolting, Orin F. *Post-Entry Training in the Public Service in Western Europe.* Chicago: International City Managers' Association, 1962, 106 pp.

A report showing how local governments in western Europe have developed post-entry training programs, the extent to which such training is provided, and how it is conducted. The study emphasizes programs for the training of administrative and executive personnel and also administrative training for professional and technical personnel who have administrative duties.

Personnel Officers Seminar: A Report. Lawrence: Governmental Research Center, University of Kansas, Annual.

A report on seminars designed for personnel officers representing a wide variety of public agencies at all levels of government and personnel managers of private firms. The goal of the seminar was "to lift the participants' interests above the routine functions of their positions and to provide stimulation and knowledge regarding new ideas, improved methods and latest techniques." The report includes presentations and summaries of discussions.

Proceedings of the Annual Short Course for Professional City Administrators. Stillwater: Business Extension Service, College of Business, Oklahoma State University, Annual.

Includes addresses and seminar proceedings of the three-day courses. Topics covered include general as well as specific aspects of city administration.

Proceedings (of) Conference on Continuing Education for Public Administrators in State, County and City

Government in California. Berkeley: Institute of Governmental Studies, University of California, 1965.

Held November 7-9, 1963, at the University of California at Davis, this "conference was called to identify the needs of state, county and city administrators for programs of continuing education, to ascertain the agencies most qualified to provide this education and to discuss the limitations and advantages of participation in such programs by institutions of higher learning." The proceedings include the agenda of the four workshops, which were the core of the conference; the summary of workshop discussion and recommendations; conference speeches, and background papers for the city, county, and state levels.

Program of Professional Development for Urban Management: A Policy Statement—1964. Chicago: International City Managers' Association, 1964, 35 pp.

Describes the goals and an action program for providing professional development and education opportunities for the Association and the profession. A summary of the Association's professional development program appears at the end of the report.

A Proposed Educational Program for Mid-Career Local and State Government Officials in the Metropolitan Detroit Region. Detroit: Metropolitan Fund, Incorporated, July, 1966, 33 pp.

A report of the Advisory Committee including background findings and recommendations and a summary of a study on the feasibility of a program for the area. (See above, McNeill, Robert J. *A Study of the Feasibility of Mid-Career Education for Local Government Employees in the Detroit Metropolitan Area*). The report contains the results of interviews with local and mid-career officials, post questionnaire interviews, a summary of studies on the nature and content of the program. The Appendix contains lists of existing programs, suitable and not suitable; characteristics of suitable programs; persons interviewed; and samples of questionnaires.

Ridley, Clarence E. "Twenty Years of Management Training: The Growth of In-Service Training Underscores the Challenge and Opportunity of the Years Ahead for Municipal Employees," *Public Management,* XXXVI (September, 1954), 194-97.

This is a general outline of the development of in-service training programs including history, current activities, and prospects.

Rosenthal, Eleanor. *Executive Development Programs for State and Local Government Administrators: Preliminary Results of a Survey.* Chicago: American Society for Public Administration, 1959, 31 pp.

The results of a survey made by means of a questionnaire sent to state and selected city personnel directors, university bureaus of public administration, and a few professional organizations. The article describes the nature and extent of programs, illustrative programs and content, sponsorship, instructional methods, and other aspects. Appendices have a partial alphabetical—by state and city—listing of programs and a copy of the questionnaire.

Schrader, George R. "Supervisory and Management Training," *Mayor and Manager,* V (November, 1962), 6, 8.

The City Manager of Mesquite, Texas tells of the training courses taken by the first and second level supervisors in his city. Included were the International City Managers' Association's course on municipal administration, courses given

by the Institute of Management of Southern Methodist University, and other specialized courses.

Second Annual Advanced Management Training Program for City Managers: Program Directory and Study Guide. Chicago: Joint Management Program Committee, International City Managers' Association, and the Center for Programs in Government Administration, University of Chicago, 1961.

The five major areas of concern are policy planning, decision-making, communications, delegation and control, and human relations and motivations. The introduction has a short description of each section.

Sessions on the Professional Development of Urban Managers, Fifty-First Annual Conference, Montreal, Canada. Chicago: International City Managers' Association, 1965.

Papers discussed at the September 22 session are "Mid-Career Education for City Managers," "Some Problems in the Development of Urban Managers," "Responsibilities for Development of Urban Administration," and "The Professional Development of Urban Managers."

Sharpe, Carleton F. "Advanced Management Training for Managers," *Public Management,* XLII (June, 1960), 125-28.

A report reviewing the growth of executive development programs in general, and the development, organization, and goals of the International City Managers' Association's Advanced Management Training Program, held May 1-7, 1960. The program function was not "to produce better practitioners or specialists, but to produce better generalists." Five areas were concentrated upon: policy planning, decision-making, communication, delegation and control, and human relations and motivation.

Stanley, David T. *Professional Personnel for the City of New York.* Washington, D.C.: The Brookings Institution, 1963, 461 pp.

Chapter eight of this book on New York City's personnel system deals with training and development, including the evaluation of a training program, the City's organizations and resources for training, in-service and outside training, executive and middle management development, the trainee programs, and city government training in general.

Stene, Edwin O. *Case Problems in City Management.* Chicago: International City Managers' Association, 1964, 153 pp.

Thirty-seven cases based on actual experiences in municipal government are grouped according to area of problem; i.e., financial control, personnel, etc. Each group of cases is preceded by a general discussion of the area and its problems.

————. *The City Manager: Professional Training and Tenure.* Lawrence: Governmental Research Center, University of Kansas, 1966, 84 pp.

This provides information on the changing roles of the city manager and insights into his training and tenure. It includes statistical tables and charts.

Stewart, Alva W. "Back to School for Tar Heel City Officials," *Public Management,* XLIX (February, 1967), 40-42.

Describes the work of the Institute of Government of the University of North Carolina and its municipal administration course which acquaints city officials with the "whole spectrum of municipal government."

Stewart, Ward, and Honey, John C. *University-Sponsored Executive Development Programs in the Public Service*. Washington, D.C.: United States Office of Education, 1966, 75 pp.

The authors bring together comprehensive, current information obtained by a nation-wide survey and indicate some trends.

Tandy, William J., and Dowey, R. S. "Speeding Up A Supervisory Training Program: How Two Professional Trainers Carried Through a Program That Indirectly Trained Over 1200 Supervisors in Less Than 2 Years," *Public Personnel Review*, XX (October, 1959), 292-95.

An outline of the background, course content, training aids, and results of the training program conducted by the new Personnel Management Division of the Civil Service Department in Los Angeles from 1957-1959.

Taylor, Bill N. "Supervisory Training Pays Off in Columbia," *Personnel Administration*, XIV (March, 1951), 26-30.

A description of the supervisory program conducted in Columbia, Missouri. It was designed to develop the supervisor as a group leader. The article focuses on the objectives and background of the program and gives a description of conferences and an evaluation of results.

The Technique of Municipal Administration, 4th ed. Chicago: International City Managers' Association, 1958, 441 pp.

This deals with the administrator's job and top-management problems and techniques.

Third Annual Supervisors Management Conference, May 6, 1961. Salem: Oregon Board of Higher Education, 1961.

Conference participants received a kit containing brief essays or pamphlets on communication, administration, interviewing, telephone personality, and research. A bibliography was included.

Training for Municipal Administrators. Chicago: International City Managers' Association, 1958, 20 pp.

A report of findings and recommendations concerning administrative training and development.

Training Program for Management Analysis: A Progress Report on the Development and Conduct of Training Programs for Management Analysis in the Municipal Government of the City of New York. New York: Division of Analysis, New York City Bureau of the Budget, October, 1950, 34 pp.

This report describes three completed training programs and plans for future programs.

University Offerings in the Career Education Awards Program: Cornell University, Harvard University, Indiana University, Princeton University, Stanford University, The University of Chicago, University of Virginia. Washington, D.C.: National Institute of Public Affairs, November, 1965, 83 pp.

A brief description of each university's program for outstanding young career public officials consisting of a year's graduate study related broadly to problems of public policy.

Vanderburg, D. Robert. "Marquette, Michigan's Management Development Program," *Mayor and Manager*, I (June, 1958), 16-18.

A brief survey of the management development program offered to the city administrators and their assistants by Marquette, Michigan.

Watt, Graham W. "How to Improve Work Methods," *Public Management*, XXXV (January, 1953), 9-10.

This article is based on the premise that increased employee output and efficiency depends upon finding better, simpler, and easier ways of doing work and concentrates on the training program developed by the Research and Budget Department of Kansas City to improve services and lower costs. The article outlines the content of the ten training sessions which emphasize distribution of work, systems analysis, and improvement of organization, office lighting, and layout.

Wolfer, D. P. "In-Service Training Covers Executive Development," *Public Management*, XLIV (March, 1962), 60-61.

In the in-service training provided for city department heads in Fort Lauderdale, Florida, all department heads meet one morning each month to "review development in modern management, keep abreast of new methods," and develop better ways of managing city operations. The training is intended for those who lack time and motivation for reading and study.

Zimmerman, Joseph F. "Worcester Conducts Training Course," *American City*, LXXVIII (April, 1962), 131.

A description of a course in supervisory techniques sponsored by the Worcester, Massachusetts Personnel Department and the local chapter of the Society for the Advancement of Management.

2. General References on Purpose, Development, Organization, and Evaluation of Training Programs

Alves, Euro, and Hardy, William R. "Evaluating Supervisory Training in Los Angeles County," *Training Directors Journal*, XVII (August, 1963), 36-40.

The authors outline specific objectives of the evaluation, describe the research based on two questionnaires, give some of the results of the latter, and make recommendations.

The Art of Supervision. Washington, D.C.: Office of Employee Development, United States Social Security Administration, 1964, 32 pp.

A report which contains the course outline, including bibliography, lesson guide, outline of visual presentation, narrative script, sample test questions, and handout material.

Bailey, Stephen K., and others. "Training for Municipal Executives," *Mayor and Manager*, VIII (November, 1965), 12-16.

With one exception, these are comments by university professors taken from papers presented before an International City Managers' Association meeting.

Baum, Bernard H., and others. "Organizational Effect of Supervisory Human Relations Training: An Evaluative Technique," *Personnel Journal,* XLVII (March, 1966), 148-52.

A technique is suggested for evaluating the effectiveness of the human relations aspects of supervisory development programs.

Beckman, R. O. *How to Train Supervisors: Manual and Outline for Determinate Discussion.* New York: Harper and Brothers, 1952, 335 pp.

A manual concerned with training techniques with special emphasis on the discussion method of training. The two main parts consist of a Manual of Procedure and Outlines for Discussion. Special features include charts, hypothetical examples of the discussion methods, and a selected bibliography on supervision, leadership, and training.

Berry, A. E. "Training for Public Service," *Municipal World,* LXXV (March, 1965), 79-81.

The need for training, the part it should play, and the most feasible procedure for training both appointed and elected officials are discussed.

Bray, F., and others. *Training Managers in the Public Services.* London: George Allen & Unwin, 1955, 84 pp.

A symposium derived from a series of lectures organized by the Royal Institute of Public Administration. The purpose was to provide an account of the schemes for training in management that had been developed in various branches of the public services, and the principles on which they were based.

Brenneman, Leroy J. "Training Supervisors," *Public Personnel Administrative Bulletin,* VII (1962), 1-2.

Described briefly are different steps to be taken in training programs; i.e., who should receive training, what kind, training resources, keeping records, and recognition of trainees.

Caldwell, Lynton K. *Leadership Behavior: Some Requirements for Leadership Training.* Washington, D.C.: Office of Career Development, United States Civil Service Commission, 1962, 39 pp.

The purpose of this publication is to integrate the information available from leadership research and theory, and to focus that information on the problem of leadership training. Topics dealt with include a leader training program, the nature of leadership, critical functions of the group, leadership training, a paradigm, a diagram of four critical leadership functions, and various technical notes.

Calkins, Robert D. "Executive Training," *Personnel Administration,* XVIII (November, 1955), 5-12.

The author discusses future needs of administration; the value of experience versus training; kinds of training that should be done by government, industry, and the universities; the necessity for analyzing training techniques; and the nature of the administrator's job. He describes an experimental program for executive training to be conducted by the Brookings Institution in Washington, D.C.

Callard, Keith B. *Advanced Administrative Training in the Public Service.* Toronto: Institute of Public Administration, 1958, 32 pp.

Describes and discusses recruitment and training for administrators with recommendations for improvement.

Conference Method Training in Management. Chicago: International City Managers' Association, 1946, 12 pp.

Designed to help city officials organize and conduct management training conferences for administrative personnel, this article includes sections on organizing the conference, conference procedures, and the conference leader's job.

Dimock, Marshall E. "Executive Development After Ten Years," *Public Administration Review,* XVIII (Spring, 1958), 91-97.

This article discusses the reasons for deficiencies in executive development, and makes suggestions for overcoming them.

Gabis, Stanley T. "What Kind of Training Should the Administrator Have?" *Special Report No. 11.* Lawrence: Governmental Research Center, University of Kansas, 1962, 8-13.

A general discussion of continuing training for administrators which includes a checklist of actions leading to better use of on-site and off-site training opportunities.

Gerletti, John D., and Black, Frank B. *Successful Supervision: A Guide for Training Supervisors.* Dubuque: William C. Brown Company, 1956, 66 pp.

The authors cover problems faced by supervisors, their present practices, and the "findings of experts."

The Human Problems of Supervision: Conference Leader's Guide. Washington, D.C.: Office of Personnel Administration, United States Department of Labor, 1961, 49 pp.

Stresses the common problems supervisors have in dealing with subordinates and assists supervisors to think through the solution to such problems.

Huttner, Ludwig, and Zimmerman, John. "Supervisory Training: The Conference Method," *Personnel,* XXXVIII (November, 1956), 250-58.

The authors deal with the reasons for the conference method, training of leaders, content of the program, conference procedures, evaluation of the program, and samples of materials used.

Korb, L. David. "How to Measure the Results of Supervisory Training," *Personnel,* XXXVIII (March, 1956), 378-91.

The author describes what can be expected from evaluation, its practical aspects, the requirements of an evaluation plan, and various methods to be used. Two sample plans are included as well as various exhibits to be used as guides in developing a plan.

_____. *Training the Supervisor—for Improved Performance, for Higher Morale, for Career Development.* Washington, D.C.: United States Civil Service Commission, September, 1956, 125 pp.

A guide on how to set up and conduct a supervisory training program. It is specific and detailed and could be applied in most situations, although prepared for use in the federal service.

Lee, Irving J., and Lee, Laura L. *Handling Barriers in Communication: Lecture-Discussions and Conferee's*

Handbook. New York: Harper and Brothers, 1957, 209 pp.

Leader's manual for conducting a lecture-discussion type of training program in communications for supervisory personnel; also includes a conferee's handbook containing the reading material and written assignments required of the participants.

Management Development at the Pre-Supervisory Level. Washington, D.C.: United States National Security Agency, 1955, 21 pp.

Covers the selection and development of supervisory personnel and provision for periodic evaluation of trainee progress. The appendix includes copies of forms used.

Matteson, Robert J. M. *Management Development for Public Administration*. New York: Institute of Public Administration, 1957, 10 pp.

Increased research into the need for broad governmental executive development is urged in this paper given at the 1957 Public Personnel Association conference.

McClure, Russell E., and others. "On-the-Job Training of Supervisory Personnel," *Public Management*, XXXV (January, 1953), 2-7.

A series of brief discussions of supervisory training, namely: "Purpose and Goals of Training" by R. E. McClure; "Inventory of Training Needs" by C. A. Miller; "Methods of Supervisory Training" by S. Matthews; "The Administration of Training" by E. Gunter; and "Appraising Training Results" by B. W. Johnson.

Miles, Raymond E., and Porter, Lyman W. "Leadership Training—Back to the Classroom?," *Personnel*, XLVIII (July-August, 1966), 27-35.

An approach to management training centered around the collection and feedback of managers' current attitudes. The authors describe, session by session, the content of a standard, two and one-half day, eight session training program using this approach and the results of a follow-up questionnaire.

Mosher, Frederick C. *A Proposed Program of Mid-Career Education for Public Administrators in Metropolitan Areas*. Washington, D.C.: National Institute of Public Affairs, December, 1965, 96 pp.

The proposed program is for university education. Part I sets forth the basic considerations which led to the development of the kind of plan developed; Part II is a concise statement of the program itself. The Appendix presents supporting materials, including preliminary syllabi of each principal topic in the basic course. The emphasis is on metropolitan problems.

Odiorne, George S. "Management Training—The Conflict Between Economics and Social Science," *Training Directors Journal*, XVIII (September, 1964), 2-10.

Discussion of the faults of early supervisory training, the different kinds of management and when to use each, teaching basics of pertinent behavior, and how training serves an economic role.

Olsen, Allan S. "Building a Management Team: The Chief Administrator's Job Is To Develop and Improve Department Head Performance and Teamwork Through Group Training," *Public Management*, XXXIV (August, 1952), 170-73.

The importance of supervisory employees to the chief administrator is stressed in this article. An approach to the training of administrative personnel is suggested, including an appraisal of training needs of department heads, a plan of self-development for training heads, group discussion training, putting in-service training into effect, and the appraisal of results.

Parker, R. S. "Executive Development in the Commonwealth Public Service," *Public Administration* (Australia), XXXIV (September, 1956), 177-98.

Discussion of the specific problems of education and formal training for higher administration. It includes sections on the role of the administrator, current provisions, and comments and recommendations on the provisions.

The Purchase and Financing of Town Highway Machinery. Albany: The Association of Towns of the State of New York, 1958, 77 pp.

An in-service training manual which discusses the law and procedures for purchasing and financing town highway machinery.

Sherwood, Frank P., and Best, Wallace H. "Supervisory Techniques: Training and Safety," *Supervisory Methods in Municipal Administration*. Chicago: International City Managers' Association, 1958, 230-48.

Covers what is training, the climate of learning, discovering training needs, planning training programs, how to instruct, and safety.

Sullivan, John W. "Increasing Computer Efficiency: Educate All Personnel," *Advanced Management Journal*, XXIV (January, 1964), 17-19.

The author points out that inefficient operation of computers is due to lack of education and training of executives, managers, and workers.

Supervision and Supervisory Training, Selected Guides and Viewpoints to Aid in Supervision and in Planning Supervisory Training. Washington, D.C.: Society for Personnel Administration, July, 1954, 44 pp.

This is a group of papers with the following titles: "Supervisory Training as a Diagnostic Instrument," "Take a Look at Supervisor Training," "The Dilemma of Personnel Administration," "What's Wrong With Supervision?," and "Important Considerations in Planning Supervisory Training."

Training for Supervisors in Employee-Management Cooperation. Washington, D.C.: United States Veterans Administration, 1963, 69 pp.

Contains a conference plan, illustrations of eight visual aids, and copies of three handouts.

3. General References on Techniques of Training

Audio-Visual Aids for Data Processing Systems. Park Ridge, Ill.: Data Processing Management Association, 1966, 20 pp.

This is designed as a guide for chapter education program chairmen. It is in two sections which (1) list films produced by manufacturers of equipment and independent producers, and (2) list addresses for ordering films.

The Case Method: A Technique of Management Development. Washington, D.C.: Society for Personnel Administration, 1957, 32 pp.

The proceedings of an all-day workshop with a diverse group of specialists from university, government, and industry serving as panelists and seminar discussion leaders.

The Conference Leader's Job in Management Training. Chicago: International City Managers' Association, 1946, 13 pp.

Gives practices used by successful conference leaders which will help the inexperienced leader to avoid common mistakes. It includes sections on the first training session, leading the discussion, and preparing for the session.

Dworkis, Martin B. "The Playback: A Technique of Management Training," *Personnel Administration,* XXV (November-December, 1962), 50-53.

A step-by-step description of a "role-playing" training technique developed by the author.

Executive Development in Action: Patterns and Techniques. Washington, D.C.: Society for Personnel Administration, 1955, 31 pp.

This topical outline gives the main trends of thought and the concepts and techniques on which there was unanimity of thinking at the First and Second Annual Institutes sponsored by the Society.

Morris, Theodore P. *Instructor's Manual for Management Development: Complete Lesson Plans for Conference Discussions,* 3rd rev. ed. Pasadena: Pasadena Personnel Department, 1954, 203 pp.

This manual is designed to include basic information on all areas of the supervisor's job, to help him perform more effectively and to provide a foundation for more advanced courses. It uses the directed conference method of teaching.

Problems for Staff Officers for Use in Management Development Classes, revised. Lansing: Michigan Civil Service Commission, 1958, 8 pp.

Problem situations with special emphasis on staff relations are presented here. Each is followed by multiple-choice list of possible reactions to or solutions of the problem.

Solem, Allen R., and others. "The Posting Problems Technique As a Basis For Training," *Personnel Administration,* XXIV (July-August, 1961), 22-31.

This article describes a management training course in which the content is determined by problems submitted by the trainees.

Staff Development; The Supervisor's Job. Revised. Washington, D.C.: Division of Personnel Management, United States Department of Health, Education and Welfare, 1963, 31 pp.

Practical information is offered concerning the following topics: helping people want to develop, ways to speed learning, tools for staff development, and the climate in which people grow.

Training Kit for Discussion Leaders. Chicago: International City Managers' Association, 1960.

The kit was designed for use in the in-service training course of the Institute for Training in Municipal Administration entitled "Supervisory Methods in Municipal Administration." The kit contains an ICMA Manual, discussion leader's guides, lesson outlines, discussion questions, case studies, bibliography, two management information service reports, and reprints and pamphlets from other sources.

C. Interns and Trainees

Administrative Trainee Program. Los Angeles: Chief Administrative Officer, Los Angeles County, September 18, 1963, 6 pp.

This report covers in some detail the recruiting, appointment, training, evaluation, and placement procedures of the county system and lists initial department assignments of trainees for a ten-year period.

Brunton, Robert L., and Besuden, William E. *Internship Training for City Management.* Chicago: International City Managers' Association, 1960, 20 pp.

This survey was designed to examine the kinds of training provided, to appraise the value of internship as a training device for city management, and to determine how city-university sponsors might further improve this kind of training. The analysis considers the historical growth of internships, goals, types of internship and university programs, city criticisms of programs, the views of interns, and the process of building a program.

Clay, Hubert and Olsen, Leif O. "Internships in the Development of People," *Personnel Journal,* XLI (June, 1961), 58-63.

This article describes a program of internship for line managers under staff tutelage which is recommended as a fundamental part of a management development effort.

"Cleveland Area Summer Internship in Public Administration," *Governmental Facts* (December 8, 1965), entire issue.

This article describes various features of the internship program in order that a maximum amount of information will be available to educational institutions and prospective 1966 student interns. It includes 1965 experience and a three-year view.

Cottrell, Edwin A. "Research and Intern Training: Scoville Pioneers in Los Angeles County," *Tax Digest,* XXVIII (May, 1950), 156-59.

A brief description is provided of the purposes, development, and achievements in local government training of the Los Angeles County Division of Administrative Research.

Davy, Thomas J., and Wagner, Donald C. "Establishing Internships," *Public Administration News,* XXXVI (June, 1958), entire issue.

Values of internships are discussed and eight characteristics of leading internship programs are described.

Detzer, Karl. "Interns at City Hall: Young Trainees, Topping Off Formal Education With Work Under City Managers, Spread Good Government," *National Municipal Review,* XLVII (November, 1958), 494-96, 525.

This article emphasizes the use of intern programs in local government by using case studies of city managers who employed what they learned from their own intern experience.

Engelbert, Ernest A. *An Evaluation of Internship and Student Training Programs in Southern California.* Los Angeles: Internship Committee, Joint College-Federal Service Council for Southern California, 1953, 80 pp.

An analysis of fifteen selected training programs reflecting different approaches at various governmental levels and variations in training procedures.

Haug, Dean Russell. *An Analysis of Administrative Internships From the Point of View of the Intern: A Critical Incident Approach.* Los Angeles: School of Public Administration, University of Southern California, January, 1953, 146 pp.

The purpose of this study was to investigate the first-hand experiences and observations of interns who had completed administrative internships in various local governments in the United States. Most of the experiences reported by interns concerned difficulties and problems encountered and were, for the most part, of an unfavorable nature. They pointed to a need for better planning of the programs being offered. Areas of greatest inadequacy seem to be those concerned with the administering of the programs.

Hollinger, Lindon S. *Building a Career Civil Service System: The Los Angeles County Internship Program.* Los Angeles: Chief Administrative Officer, Los Angeles County, August 12, 1964, 6 pp.

One of the oldest internship programs, established in 1933, is described here. Figures are included on the present occupations of the 131 graduates of the program.

The Internship in Public Affairs. San Francisco: Coro Foundation, 1954, 4 pp.

"The Internship in Municipal Affairs sponsored by Coro Foundation of San Francisco is given to twelve carefully selected individuals annually who are preparing for careers in public affairs. The internship requires the full-time participation of each intern (7¼ hours per day, 5 days per week). For the purposes of selection and analysis, the Foundation obtains and maintains a written record of the intern's previous education and training. Grades are not given nor are specific credits granted. Upon completion, the intern receives a certificate certifying his satisfactory performance."

Internship Programs in States, Cities, and Counties: A Survey. New York: National Civil Service League, 1956, 19 pp.

The survey indicates that internships, once tried, are welcomed by government and participating universities. The primary retarding force would seem to be the reluctance of appropriating bodies to spend money on internships.

Jenkins, Wilbur L. "Why Not a Personnel Technician Intern Program?" *Public Personnel Review,* XVIII (July, 1957), 174-77.

This article gives an outline for improving relationships between the personnel department and operating departments based on the assumption that in many respects personnel technicians are the least prepared of all professions to engage in the important work assigned to them and that a personnel technician must experience the problems, frustrations, and rewards derived from the particular jobs for which he selects personnel.

"Management Seminars Conducted by Assistants and Interns," *Public Management,* XLVI (May, 1964), 114-15.

A description of the operation of seminars and their results.

Miller, Jerome E. *A Suggested Training Program for the Position of Administrative Intern in the City of Tucson.* Tucson: Budget and Research Division, Tucson Department of Administration, 1964, 30 pp.

A detailed outline of a program suggested for Tucson. Information received in answer to a questionnaire sent to other cities is summarized.

Morris, Robert B. "Trainees for City Management," *Public Management,* XXXV (August, 1953), 174-78.

The development of an administrative training program for the Village of Glencoe, Illinois is outlined in this article. It emphasizes the advantages of sound educational training for the interns and suggests materially increasing the work output of all village departments.

Needed—A Management-Training Program for New York City. New York: Committee on City Affairs, New York Chamber of Commerce, March 7, 1957, 10 pp.

An argument for an administrative intern program in New York City which also presents disadvantages and sources of opposition to such a program.

Opportunities for Administrative Internships in Public Administration in Northeast Ohio. Cleveland: Cleveland Governmental Research Institute, 1963, 7 pp.

A questionnaire to determine interest in an administrative intern program was distributed in 1962 by the Cleveland Chapter of the American Society for Public Administration. Results are summarized and evaluated, and conclusions from the information received are presented in this publication. A copy of the questionnaire is attached.

The Pasadena Internship Plan. Pasadena: Pasadena Personnel Department, no date, 18 pp.

Half-time internships are offered to qualified college students. This publication describes the program generally and lists the specific departments and duties to which interns may be assigned. Assignments are on a rotational basis, lasting from one to six weeks in any one department.

Powers, Stanley. "Professional Manpower Needed: Municipal Intern Programs," *Public Management,* XLVIII (March-April, 1966), 108-12.

This article briefly summarizes the general development of intern programs to date considering various types of programs and the general methods of implementation. The author concludes with suggestions for improving organization and direction to overcome existing shortcomings in these programs.

Rizos, E. John. "City Hall Internships for Management," *Public Management,* XXXVIII (January, 1956), 8-10.

A general overview of the objectives and advantages of co-operation between municipal officials and universities in developing intern programs in city management.

Sheil, Marion D. "Cuyahoga County Library Tackles the Recruitment Problem in a Practical Way, With Its Newly-Developed Intern Program," *Library Journal,* LXXX (June 1, 1962), 2093-095.

The plan described combines study in a nearby school of library science with work in the library in a specific professional position whereby the student can obtain his Master's Degree in Library Science in three years.

Summer Internship in Public Administration, Cleveland, Ohio: A Progress Report. Cleveland: Cleveland Governmental Research Institute, February, 1964, 45 pp.

The summer internship program consists primarily of "purposeful work assignments" and seminars. It is designed to supplement academic curricula and is not a summer school. Assignments are made to local government agencies and associations, and to federal installations. The background and organization of the program are presented in detail.

"Summer Internship in Public Administration," *Ohio Cities and Villages,* XII (February, 1964), 7-10.

A ten-week program in the Cleveland area provides training opportunities in public agencies for superior undergraduate college students. Details about recruitment, kind of student, program operation, and student's work experience are given.

"Summer Internship in Public Administration," *Ohio Cities and Villages,* XIV (July, 1966), 18-20. Reprinted from *Governmental Facts,* December 8, 1965. This article describes various features of a ten-week internship program in Cleveland for superior undergraduate col-

lege students after its third year of operation, and includes statistics for the period.

Thompson, Herbert W., Giltner, Robert E., and Andrews, Marvin A. *Training for the Public Service: Council-Management Government; the Program and Reports on its Operation.* Urbana: Institute of Government and Public Affairs, University of Illinois, 1955, 18 pp.

The description of the program is followed by narrative reports on the experiences of each of three interns.

Urie, John M., and Reese, Howard L. "Phoenix Administrative Intern Plan Proves Aid to City Department," *Western City,* XXXI (July, 1955), 52, 71.

This article is a brief and general description of the Phoenix program begun in 1950.

Vickers, S. E. "Improving Employee Performance," *Proceedings of the Fifty-Eighth Annual Public Works Congress.* Chicago: American Public Works Association, 1952, 40-44.

A description and discussion of the techniques of internships, rotation training, and administrative assistantships.

Watson, James R. "Internships for Public Service Training," *State Government,* XXX (March, 1957), 67-69.

Less than a third of the states and smaller proportions of counties and cities surveyed by the National Civil Service League have adopted internships as part of their training or recruitment systems. The author summarizes the results of the survey after discussing the purpose of internships, their early development, and policy frameworks in which they can thrive.

Wilson, Celianna I. "Professional Internship: A Program and a Proposal," *Library Journal,* LXXXI (June 1, 1963), 2201-205.

The author, Personnel Librarian at the Ohio State University Library, describes its first internship program and proposes for libraries an internship program modeled after that of the medical profession.

Woodford, Dorothy. "Public Administration Intern Program," *Municipal Finance,* XXIII (May, 1951), 150-52.

This article deals with the approach taken by Kansas City, Missouri toward effective finance personnel management. The focus of the article is on the reasons for using interns in municipal government, how to recruit qualified interns, and the procedures for conducting an intern program.

Part III
Training Personnel in Functional Fields

A. Corrections, Juvenile Delinquency, Probation, and Parole

1. Surveys, Descriptions, and Analyses of Local Training Needs, Resources, and Programs

Administration and Staff Training in Institutions for Juvenile Delinquency: A Report Based on a Workshop. Washington, D.C.: United States Children's Bureau, 1959, 47 pp.

Partial contents are as follows: "Staff Training from the Superintendent's Perspective," "Training as Staff Problem Solving," and "Administration of a Staff Problem Solving Training Program."

Charting the Course: Proceedings of a Meeting . . . June 27-28, 1966. Washington, D.C.: Joint Commission on Correctional Manpower and Training, September, 1966, 57 pp.

The Joint Commission on Correctional Manpower and Training, composed of representatives of ninety-five organizations, met to hear outstanding speakers whose talks are included in this report. In addition, the report covers each of the Task Forces, the scope of the charges to them, and a short description of the work each Task Force planned to do.

Cincinnati Demonstration of Inter-Agency Training, A Project of the Committee on Juvenile Delinquency Control . . . Supplement No. 1, Handbook for Trainees. Cincinnati: Community Health and Welfare Council, 1964, 112 pp.

This is the handbook of training materials used by the trainees of the demonstration project. It includes working papers; a description of the area selected for the project, training goals, and expectations of the participating organizations; descriptions of the participating organizations; descriptions of the participating agencies' health and welfare services in the area; and case histories used as study material by the trainees.

Cincinnati Demonstration for Inter-Agency Training, A Project of the Committee on Juvenile Delinquency Control . . . Final Report, May 1963-May 1964. Cincinnati: Community Health and Welfare Council, 1964, 55 pp.

"The purpose of the demonstration has been to train police, juvenile court workers, school personnel, and public welfare staff to work more effectively with youth who may become delinquent." The workshop type of in-service training was used. The program began with a two day institute at a location away from the work location. This was followed by small group sessions of ninety minutes each twice weekly for six weeks and then once weekly for six weeks.

Crites, M. Mark. "Group Counseling for Probations and Staff," *Crime and Delinquency,* XI (October, 1965), 355-59.

By providing continuing training and consultation with the staff psychologist, the Sacramento County (California) Probation Department developed a successful program of group counseling for probationers.

Curriculum of Training for Supervisors, Professional and Pre-Professional Caseworkers and Group Workers, Street Club Workers, Volunteers and Parents in the Prevention-Treatment of Juvenile Delinquency and Multi-Problem Families. New York: New York City Youth Board, 1961, 45 pp.

This is the curriculum of workshops, seminars, etc., offered by the Youth Board "designed to strengthen the professionally trained in the treatment of internal pressures and conflicts and to develop the untrained to render with assurance and adequacy the necessary services to counteract, modify or eliminate external pressures."

Delinquency Control and Prevention Training for Police Officers; Digest of Findings. Madison: Bureau of

Government, Extension Division, University of Wisconsin, December, 1959, 6 pp.

A digest of principal findings and some general conclusions based on the data of a study initiated by the Bureau in June, 1959 which sought to evaluate the general effectiveness of the juvenile delinquency prevention training program conducted during 1956-59, especially the Two-Week Delinquency Control Course for Law Enforcement Officers.

Functional Categories of Training Projects, Juvenile Delinquency and Youth Offenses Control Act: Training Projects Being Supported Under the Juvenile Delinquency and Youth Offenses Control Act. . . Washington, D.C.: Office of Juvenile Delinquency and Youth Development, United States Welfare Administration, April, 1965, 179 pp.

A brief description is included for each project.

Gernert, Paul J. "Manpower for Corrections, Probation and Parole," *Pennsylvania Chiefs of Police Association Bulletin,* XXVII (Fall, 1966), 11, 27.

The Chairman of the Pennsylvania Board of Parole reports on how his Board can support provisions of 1965 state legislation, in regard to in-service training, but lacks the manpower to execute them.

Giardini, G. I. "Personnel Training in Parole and Probation," *Prison Journal,* XL (April, 1960), 25-27.

A brief survey of the in-service training program of the Pennsylvania Board of Parole.

Gilman, Merritt Curtis. "Problems and Progress in Staff Training," *Crime and Delinquency,* XII (July, 1966), 254-60.

The progress made in training programs for police, probation, and parole officers, judges, and institutional personnel is discussed and the objectives of orientation and in-service training programs are analyzed in this article.

————. *Training for Juvenile Probation Officers.* Washington, D.C.: United States Department of Health, Education and Welfare, 1962, 78 pp.

A report of a workshop discussion held at Haven Hill Lodge, Michigan, in June, 1960, which indicates the differences of opinion among the participants at several points as to what constitutes probation.

Gilman, Merritt Curtis, and Low, Alice M. *Training for Juvenile Probation Officers; A Workshop Report.* Washington, D.C.: United States Children's Bureau, 1963, 78 pp.

This workshop on training problems considered the legal and social components of probation, the role of the probation officer, what he needs to know, and his education and training.

Greenblatt, Bernard. "Staff and Training for Juvenile Law Enforcement in Urban Police Departments," *Juvenile Delinquency: Facts and Facets.* Washington, D.C.: United States Government Printing Office, 1960.

This article is based on information obtained from a nationwide questionnaire survey conducted by the United States Children's Bureau. It covers staff, number and kinds of units, educational requirements for staff, and kinds of training.

Interim Progress Report, Training Demonstration Grant, July 1, 1963 to June 30, 1964. St. Louis: Institute for Delinquency Control, School of Social Service, St. Louis University, no date.

This project is aimed at developing methods and curricula content to improve the training of juvenile correctional officers. The report describes in some detail the content and methods employed in two training institutes and follow-up workshops, and a probation training project. Evaluations of the programs are also included. The institutes were intended for juvenile correctional officers; the probation training project, for social service graduate students.

An Interstate Approach to Juvenile Delinquency, Research and Training: A Survey. Boulder: Western Interstate Commission for Higher Education, August, 1963, 92 pp.

This is the "first comprehensive survey of training and research needs in the West. It has examined the role that higher education might play in meeting some of the training needs for persons working in these fields of endeavor and in developing new knowledge." Information includes university programs, and the educational background of workers, with suggestions for improvement, including in-service training. California is covered in a separate section. The final chapter is entitled "Guidelines for New Regional Programs and Proposed Educational Demonstrations."

Ives, Jane K. "Basic Training for Probation Officers," *Social Work,* VIII (July, 1963), 51-58.

Three training courses are used to illustrate a major problem of training—selecting subject matter and focus to fit the readiness of trainees.

Miller, Fred H. "Training at the Local Level for Correctional Service," *Prison Journal,* XL (April, 1960), 16-19.

A brief survey of the services offered by the Public Service Institute of the Pennsylvania Department of Public Instruction.

New Ideas in Training: Training Programs for Youth Workers Being Supported Under the Juvenile Delinquency Act of 1961. Washington, D.C.: United States President's Committee on Juvenile Delinquency and Youth Crime, 1963, 14 pp.

"The over-all goal of the training program being carried out under the Juvenile Delinquency Act is to provide more and better training for people who work with delinquents and potential delinquents." Mention is made of representative projects and the background against which they have been developed.

Noble, Henry J. *The Center for Correctional Training and the New York City Department of Correction.* New York: Center for Correctional Training, New York City Department of Correction, December 16, 1965, 10 pp.

Traces the development of correctional training programs in New York City from the organization of a two weeks training school on Rikers Island in 1939. Courses are conducted, sometimes jointly, for the uniformed personnel and the professional staff. Special courses and lectures are also offered at the individual institutions and to suit specific situations.

O'Leary, Vincent. "A National Training Program for Parole Officials," *State Government,* XXXVII (Spring, 1964), 114-17.

Description of a series of training sessions in different regions of the country, their inception and organization, their basic character, and the promising developments emerging from them.

Pursuit, Dan G. "Training for Juvenile Delinquency Control," *Police Chiefs News,* XVII (January, 1950), 19-24.

Provides general information on the Delinquency Control Institute at the University of Southern California—its purpose, organization, and curriculum.

Report and Miscellaneous Papers. New York: Special Committee on Probation Services in the Courts, City of New York, March 13, 1956, 13 pp.

A report covering a brief history of probation in New York, probation training and recruitment, and the task of the Probation Officer. The specific program presented calls for a "work-study program leading to a Master's Degree in social work for incumbent probation officers" beginning with those in supervisory positions.

Roebuck, Julian, and Zelhart, Paul. "The Problem of Educating the Correctional Practitionery," *Journal of Criminal Law, Criminology, and Police Science,* LVI (March, 1965), 45-53.

This article discusses the issue of professionalization, the controversy over academic preparation, and gives the results of a poll which the authors took of 141 correctional specialists concerning their views on education for corrections.

Russell, Bernard. "Current Training Needs in the Field of Juvenile Delinquency," *Juvenile Delinquency: Facts and Facets.* Washington, D.C.: United States Government Printing Office, 1960.

The author deals with the need for training in the field of juvenile delinquency for judges, institutional workers, and police. He also covers sources of additional workers, and makes recommendations.

Studt, Elliot, and Russell, Bernard. *Staff Training for Personnel in Institutions for Juvenile Delinquents: Report of a Workshop.* Washington, D.C.: United States Children's Bureau, 1958, 56 pp.

The workshop was set up to develop methods utilizing the skills and knowledge of both professional and experienced non-professional personnel and to make more effective use of training.

Summaries of Training Projects, Juvenile Delinquency and Youth Offenses Control Act: Training Projects Being Supported Under the Juvenile Delinquency and Youth Offenses Control Act. . . Washington, D.C.: Office of Juvenile Delinquency and Youth De-velopment, United States Welfare Administration, April, 1965, 167 pp.

A brief outline of purpose, method, and scope is included for each project.

Swab, Robert D., Jr. "County Level Institutes on Police Handling of Juveniles: Institutes Equip Police to Better Prevent and Control Juvenile Delinquency as Part of Planned Community Effort," *Bulletin,* XXIII (Fall, 1962), 21, 31.

County institutes are sponsored by the local juvenile courts in cooperation with state offices and the Pennsylvania Chiefs of Police Association. The twenty-hour basic course is designed to benefit police administrators and personnel in providing increased services to children and their families and to prepare officers for advanced training in juvenile police work for departments large enough to have specialists or units.

"Training for Probation and Parole Work," *National Probation and Parole Association Journal* (July, 1956), 193-259.

This is a group of articles covering professional education for the correctional field; criminology for probation and parole officers, problems of the social worker in probation and parole work, student placement in probation work, training for delinquency control at the University of Minnesota, a state in-service training program, and some experiences in training in a county probation department.

Training Personnel for Work with Juvenile Delinquents. Washington, D.C.: United States Children's Bureau, 1954, 90 pp.

Experts on juvenile delinquency were called together to comment on papers which had been prepared on the problem of providing education and training for personnel working with juvenile delinquents.

Wall, John. "Juvenile Probation and Parole: Emerging Needs for Staff Training and Development," *Louisiana Welfare,* XXIII (April-July, 1962), 16-19.

The summer training program for juvenile probation and parole officers given by the Tulane University School of Social Work is described.

Wolke, Michael S. "Police Need Training in Problems of Youth," *Law and Order,* VII (October, 1959), 33-34.

The author advocates greater emphasis on training in "the science of human relations" for all law enforcement personnel with special emphasis on "crime prevention work."

2. General References on Purpose, Development, Organization, and Evaluation of Training Programs

Chenault, Price. "Structuring an In-Service Training Program for Correctional Workers," *Journal of Correctional Education,* XII (July, 1960), 3-11.

The author outlines a complete set of procedures for determining training objectives and needs, and lists some of the more important factors that should be considered when conducting an in-service training program.

In-Service Training Standards for Prison Custodial Officers. New York: Committee of Personnel Standards and Training, American Prison Association, 1951, 64 pp.

Part I covers in-service training for the adult correctional institution—including objectives, organization, space, equipment and budget, and methods. Part II covers qualifications and duties of custodial officers and outlines and describes ten basic training courses.

Ives, Jane K. "Basic Training for Probation Officers," *Social Work,* VIII (July, 1963), 51-58.

The author discusses the types of training programs likely to have practical applications for probation-work trainees and analyzes the various stages of the trainees' development during which a particular type of training is likely to be most acceptable and practical.

————. "The Learner in Probation Work," *Crime and Delinquency,* XI (July, 1965), 239-48.

Some of the more common problems encountered by trainees and students in probation work are identified and the proper actions that training supervisors should take are suggested.

Manual of Correctional Standards. Washington, D.C.: American Correctional Association, 1966, 642 pp.

Chapter 10—"Personnel Management"—in this basic manual includes selection and training standards, first in outline form, followed by discussion of each item in the outline.

The information is applicable to correctional institutions generally, including local facilities, although primarily focused on prisons.

Newman, Charles L. *Education and Training for the Field of Corrections.* Louisville: Kent School of Social Work, University of Louisville, October 1, 1964, 14 pp.

A position paper presented at a training institute on education and training for police and correctional personnel, which discusses in-service training, staff development, and pre-service training. The emphasis is on the last.

Swab, Robert D., Jr. "Police Juvenile Services Curricular Needs For In-Service Training," *Pennsylvania Chiefs of Police Association Bulletin,* XXVI (Summer, 1965), p. 12, 28-29.

Detailed outlines and suggestions to be considered in establishing a juvenile services program are presented. The outlines cover scope and objectives, determination of needs, resource materials, instructors, curriculum content, objectives, and evaluation and appraisal.

Taylor, Edward M., and McEachern, Alexander W. "Needs and Directions in Probation Training," *Federal Probation,* XXX (March, 1966), 18-24.

Discussion of the need for nationwide research and training programs for probation and tentative suggestions about the form and content of such programs.

B. Finance and Recording Officers

1. Assessors

Appraisal Short Course. . . Salem: Oregon State Tax Commission, 1964.

This is an outline of material for the intermediate and advanced sections. It is co-sponsored by Oregon State University.

The Assessment and Appraisal of South Dakota Real Estate: A Syllabus. Vermillion: Governmental Research Bureau, University of South Dakota, 1960, 108 pp.

This study guide for South Dakota assessing officers covers theories, principles, and practices of appraising city, urban, and farm real estate. It also covers cost, income, and depreciation estimates. It was prepared for use in conjunction with the annual schools held for assessing officials.

Assessors' School. Minneapolis: Center for Continuation Study, University of Minnesota.

This publication includes some of the addresses made at the school's three-day program which varies from year to year but generally includes sessions on fundamentals of assessing, advanced procedures; residential and commercial property; and urban, metropolitan, and rural property.

Assessors' Training Program. Albany: New York State Board of Equalization and Assessment, November, 1959, 140 pp.

A basic course in assessment roll preparation, assessment law, and real property evaluation. The material includes

charts and thirty-five millimeter color slides which are used in conjunction with demonstration approvals of a residence, a small farm, and a small commercial property.

The Certified Assessment Evaluation Program of the International Association of Assessing Officers. Chicago: International Association of Assessing Officers, 1964, 25 pp.

This brochure, prepared for the candidates for the professional designation, the Certified Assessment Evaluator, includes chapters on the objectives, application, written examination, and suggested study material.

Cherney, Richard A., Clopper, Simon, Baran, Edward S., and Reock, Ernest C., Jr. "Training and Education," *Assessment Administration: Papers Presented at the Twenty-Ninth International Conference on Assessment Administration, Chicago, Illinois, October 20-23, 1963.* Chicago: International Association of Assessing Officers, 1964, 51-73.

Papers presented were "The Profession's Responsibility for Training and Education"; "The IAAO Program for Training and Education"; "Recruiting New Assessing Personnel and Their Training"; and "College and University Participation in Assessors' Training Programs."

Clopper, Simon, Purnell, Robert L., and Rose, J. T., Sr. "In-Service Training," *Assessment Administration: Papers Presented at the International Conference on Assessment Administration, October 11-14,*

1959, Philadelphia. Chicago: International Association of Assessing Officers, 1960, 132-46.

Minimum requirements for a formal school are listed, and statewide programs in Maryland and Michigan are discussed. The Chesterfield County and Virginia statewide programs are also described.

Course Outline and Material for the Seven Regional Training Institutes on Tax Assessment, 1954. Austin: League of Texas Municipalities, 1954, 78 pp.

This was developed for the use of all persons attending institutes so they could more easily follow the work as it was presented and frame questions. The 1954 institutes were intended as the first step in the establishment of a comprehensive in-service training program.

Deeb, Michael S. "The Virginia Assessors' Institute: Program for Professional Development," *University of Virginia Newsletter,* XLII (January 15, 1966), entire issue.

A brief study of the history, objectives, and procedures of the organization and development of the annual Virginia Assessors' Institute which is co-sponsored by the Virginia Association of Assessing Officers and the Institute of Government of the University of Virginia.

Dietsch, John. "Organizing an Assessors' School," *Assessment Administration in Massachusetts; Proceedings of the Ninth Annual School for Massachusetts Assessors, August 18-21, 1964.* Amherst: Bureau of Government Research, University of Massachusetts, April, 1965, 12-13.

The operation of an assessors' school in Bristol County is discussed briefly.

In-Service Training Course for Assessors and Tax Collectors. Salem: Assessment and Taxation Division, Oregon State Tax Commission, Annual.

This publication includes lectures given at the five district lecture-seminar sessions. The 1947 sessions were the first course which was an orientation. They were followed by specialized and technical courses and instruction in appraisal and in administrative work in 1948 and subsequent years.

In-Service Training for Assessors. Chicago: National Association of Assessing Officers, 1946, 48 pp.

The guides which should be followed in in-service training programs for assessors are suggested in this report. Sections of the report include: training in general, present training activities, classification of training activity, methods of instruction, basic course, advanced course, short course or institute, meetings, and conferences, and organizing a school. The report also offers a series of outlines of training courses.

In-Service Training for Assessors and Assistants. Sacramento: Association of County Assessors, September, 1943, 33 pp.

Includes types of in-service training, adaptation of the various methods, procedures and techniques, and a course of study and material.

"In-Service Training Provided for Under National Housing Act," *Assessor's News Letter,* XXXI (April, 1965), 49-50.

The National Housing Act of 1964 is interpreted in this article as a basis for the allocation of federal funds for the in-service training of tax assessors.

Murray, William G., and Bivens, Gordon E. "Clinics, Bench Marks, and Improved Assessments," *National Tax Journal,* V (December, 1952), 370-75.

This article is a study of a clinic in which 142 assessors participated by making individual appraisals of selected properties of different types and then comparing their appraisals for each property with the average of the group.

Patteson, Samuel A., Jr., Gillis, Bruce C., Purnell, Robert L., and Christensen, Carl C. "Improvement of In-Service Training Programs," *Assessment Administration, Papers Presented at the Twenty-Seventh International Conference Assessment Administration, Montreal, Quebec, October 8-11, 1961.* Chicago: International Association of Assessing Officers, 1962, 139-50.

Assessment training programs in Virginia, South Dakota, Michigan, and Minnesota are discussed in some detail.

Proceedings of the . . . Annual Institute for Assessing Officers. New Brunswick: Bureau of Government Research, Rutgers University, Annual.

These proceedings are based on manuscripts and on tape recordings which have been edited and reviewed. They do not include for 1957 the lectures delivered as part of the Basic Program which was designed for new assessors and devoted to fundamentals of municipal tax assessing. The 1959 and 1960 Proceedings contain only presentations made during the most advanced of the three programs offered simultaneously.

Proceedings of the Annual School for Massachusetts Assessors. Amherst: Bureau of Government Research, University of Massachusetts, 1960-64.

The proceedings cover speeches and topical lectures. In 1964 they included the transcript of a mock appellate tax board trial.

Proceedings of the Annual Short Course for Assessing Officers. Ann Arbor: Institute of Public Administration, University of Michigan, 1964.

The proceedings include addresses given at the course, introductory remarks, question and answer periods, and comments. Several speeches, too difficult to adapt for publication, have been omitted.

Proceedings of the Annual Virginia Assessors' Institute. Charlottesville: Bureau of Public Administration, University of Virginia, Annual.

The basic purpose of the Institute during its first five-year, long-range plan was to present systematically most of the knowledge which appraisers and assessing officers should have, and the proceedings included the major content of the Institute program annually beginning with the 1961 Institute. The 1967 issue is the second in a series containing only new and advanced topics as provided by the second five-year, long-range program for the Institute.

Proceedings of the Fourteenth Annual Short Course for Assessing Officers. Ann Arbor: Institute of Public Administration, University of Michigan, 1960, 185 pp.

A report on a course for Michigan assessing officers which includes addresses, discussions on aspects of assessing, and examination questions and answers.

Proceedings of the . . . Indiana Assessment Institute. Indianapolis: Indiana Board of Tax Commissioners, 1957.

Except for formal addresses, the Proceedings are presented as summary reports. They include several panel discussions and an appendix consisting of various lists giving assessment information by state plus a section on mobile home taxes in Indiana.

Proceedings—Institute for Municipal Assessors. Madison: League of Wisconsin Municipalities, Annual.

The Proceedings cover most of the papers presented at each annual institute. They are conducted by the Assessors Section of the League in cooperation with the State Department of Taxation.

Proceedings of the School for Tax Assessors. Boulder: Bureau of Governmental Research and Service, University of Colorado, 1961.

The Proceedings cover lectures, demonstrations, seminar problems, some examinations, and miscellaneous information pertaining to the annual schools.

Proceedings: Short Course for Illinois Assessing Officials. . . . Urbana: Institute of Government and Public Affairs, University of Illinois, 1957.

The Proceedings include lectures given and comments made during the course, shortened and edited for publication.

Program and Proceedings of the Annual School for South Dakota Assessing Officers. Vermillion: Governmental Research Bureau, University of South Dakota, Annual.

A written record of the manuscript papers and tape recordings on assessments, and appraisal methods and techniques presented during school sessions. The purpose of the school was to develop knowledge and sharpen techniques and procedures.

Qualified Tax Assessors for New Jersey: Report of a Committee to Study the Training of Tax Assessors in New Jersey. New Brunswick: Division of Taxation, State of New Jersey, October, 1964, 36 pp.

This report suggests a list of desirable qualifications for assessors and a comprehensive training program. It proposes that the latter be linked with a certification procedure and a tenure plan for competent assessors.

Shannon, Francis John. "Assessment Improvement Program in Kentucky," *National Tax Journal,* III (September, 1950), 233-41.

The causes of tax assessment inequalities that led to a reform movement in Kentucky are discussed in this article. A program of in-service training for the technical staff, local assessment representatives, and local assessors was one of several steps taken.

Syllabus for Training Course for Assessing Officials. Chicago: International Association of Assessing Officers, 1966, 61 pp.

A comprehensive outline of the appraisal process using the three approaches to value: cost, income, and market. Includes chapters on business relations, maps, construction components, sample problems, and rating references. Designed as a teaching guide for instructors and a syllabus for students attending assessors' training seminars sponsored by the International Association of Assessing Officers.

Trainee Education Program: Personal Property. Los Angeles: Los Angeles County Office of Assessor, 1965, 199 pp.

The Introduction consists of instructions for conducting the trainee appraiser program, an outline of the four phases of the training, some references to sources of assessment law, and summaries of relevant judicial decisions. The balance of the material is a topical outline of each session, period by period, and a schedule.

2. Finance Officers

Chase, Reed H. "Eight Proved Principles for Training Personnel," *Purchasing,* XXXVI (June, 1954), 73-74, 292, 294, 296.

Eight training factors which will influence an employee are listed in chronological order in this article.

Compilation and Digest: 1961 Municipal Clerks and Finance Officers Institute. Santa Fe: Municipal League of New Mexico, May 31, 1961, 46 pp.

This compilation and digest consists of summaries, outlines, or complete talks prepared by the program participants. It does not include material discussed during the question and answer periods.

DaCosta, Robert C. "Training Program Aids Public Officials," *Tennessee Government,* IX (September-October, 1950), 1 and 3.

A report on a series of regional conferences held in Tennessee for different local government groups—municipal finance officers, recreation board members, and Tennessee Rural Electric Cooperative Trustees.

Fourth Annual Work Shop Conference of City Clerks and Finance Officers Division, September 15, 17, 1958, Springfield, Missouri. Springfield: Missouri Department of Finance, October, 1958, 32 pp.

This publication includes addresses on "Duties of a City Clerk," "Financial Reports Records," and "Initial Steps in Setting Up of Zoning Regulations." Each address is followed by a panel discussion.

Goldrick, M. D. "The Training and Development of Senior Administrators in Canadian Municipal Government," *Canadian Public Administration,* VI (June, 1963), 156-220.

In the section relating to development of professional standards are descriptions of training programs for clerks and treasurers arranged by province. This is preceded by a detailed description of local government in Canada and its officials, particularly clerks and treasurers. Included also are the responses to a questionnaire about the same officials.

Gotherman, J. E. "In-Service Training for Municipal Personnel," *Ohio Cities and Villages,* VIII (November, 1960), 348, 352.

Detailed description of a course in municipal finance administration which was given for department heads and personnel of the City of Dayton, Ohio and was based on the group training correspondence course of the International City Managers' Association. Other training programs of that organization are recommended.

Greene, Wilfred A. "Training for Municipal Employees in Canada," *Municipal Finance,* XXIII (May, 1951), 143-47.

An overview of in-service training programs throughout Canada for the purpose of emphasizing the value of in-service training for employees in assisting the administration in overcoming deficiencies in service. The points covered include developing a training program, the implementation of the program in Canada, and a sample syllabus.

Harrington, U. J. "In-Service Training in Nova Scotia," *Municipal Finance,* XXIII (May, 1951), 163-67.

The author deals with Nova Scotia's approach to in-service training for municipal finance personnel and includes conditions necessitating inception of training, subjects discussed in training courses, and evaluation of success.

Institute for Colorado Municipal Clerks and Finance Officers, . . . Proceedings. Boulder: Bureau of Continuation Education, Department of Political Science, University of Colorado, Annual.

A summary of presentations made at the Institute including the more informative questions and answers.

Kilpatrick, Wylie. "How Florida Officials View Their Training Course," *Municipal Finance,* XXIII (May, 1951), 155-58.

A description of a successful short course training program together with observations useful to others in planning such a training program.

Ludwig, C. C. "The Minnesota Municipal Finance Short Course," *Municipal Finance,* XXIII (May, 1951), 159-60.

This article briefly outlines the eight-year history of Minnesota's Municipal Finance Officer's Short Course held annually at the University of Minnesota's Center for Continuation Study.

McQuilken, John. "Financial In-Service Training in San Diego," *Municipal Finance,* XXIII (May, 1951), 147-49.

A brief description of the steps taken by the city of San Diego, California in earning its reputation for good financial administration.

Municipal Finance Administration. Chicago: International City Managers' Association, 1962, 519 pp.

One of a series of books dealing with various fields of municipal administration, this volume on municipal finance administration is used as the text in an in-service training course offered by the Institute for Training in Municipal Administration.

Nowak, Edward J. "Organizing a Finance Officers Training Institute," *Municipal Finance,* XXIII (May, 1951), 161-62.

A report on the procedures followed by the Michigan Finance Officers to plan and organize a two-day conference for finance officers throughout the state.

Papers Presented at County Finance School. Albany: New York State Department of Audit and Control, Annual.

Contains the papers relative to county finance in New York State presented at the annual school sponsored by the County Officers Association and County Treasurers and Finance Officers Association with the cooperation of the New York State Department of Audit and Control.

Papers Presented at Training School for Fiscal Officers and Municipal Clerks of Cities and Villages. Albany: New York State Department of Audit and Control, Annual.

Contains the papers relative to municipal finance in New York State presented at the annual school sponsored by the Conference of Mayors and Other Municipal Officials of the State of New York, New York State Society of Municipal Finance Officers, and New York State Association of City and Village Clerks in cooperation with the New York State Department of Audit and Control.

Proceedings of the Annual Wyoming Treasurer's School. Laramie: Division of Adult Education and Community Service, University of Wyoming, Annual.

The school is an intensive training course for county treasurers and others professionally interested in public finance. The Proceedings contain the papers presented at the school and cover a variety of topics.

Proceedings of the County Auditor's Institute. Austin: Institute of Public Affairs, University of Texas, Annual.

An institute designed to acquaint participants with the latest information and techniques. Programs usually consist of formal presentations by instructors and related workshop discussions. The proceedings contain either all of or the principal papers presented. In some years illustrated material used in workshop sessions is included.

"The Professor, the P. A. and the Purchasing Profession: Local Associations Team Up With Michigan State University in a Cooperative Effort. The Result: An Education Program That Can't Be Beat," *Purchasing,* XLIV (February 3, 1958), 88-89.

Cooperative efforts of local purchasing agents, associations, and Michigan State University to integrate theory and practice in purchasing.

Skillman, George C. "Municipal Finance Administration," *Municipal Finance,* XXIII (May, 1951), 153-55.

A description of the use of the organized departmental class as a means of training personnel. Focuses on how such a class is organized, conducted, and integrated with other training programs.

Tax Collection in Towns. Albany: The Association of Towns of the State of New York, 1964, 74 pp.

This training manual was prepared by the staff of the Association as part of its program of education and in-service training of town officers. Topics covered include the tax collecting officer, records, petty cash, the tax roll and warrant, public notice, office hours, tax bills, tax receipts, collection procedures, return of unpaid taxes to county treasurer, settlement with county treasurer, reports, additional collecting duties, and relations with the public.

The Town Budget System. Albany: The Association of Towns of the State of New York, 1960, 104 pp.

Prepared by the staff of the Association as part of its program of education and in-service training of town officers, this manual discusses town budget procedures, law, and forms.

Warner, Kenneth O. "Principles and Standards of In-Service Training," *Municipal Finance,* XXIII (May, 1951), 139-42.

An authoritative article on the need for, principles of, and approaches to training with emphasis on in-service training.

Wilcox, Robert F. "Practical Use of Student Trainees in Finance Departments," *Municipal Finance,* XXVII (November, 1954), 59-65.

A discussion of an approach toward securing and training better administrative personnel is presented in this article. It includes not only an overview of what functions intern programs have but also a five-point recommendation of the essentials of a sound student trainee program.

Woodford, Dorothy. "Public Administration Intern Program," *Municipal Finance,* XXIII (May, 1951), 150-52.

This article deals with the approach taken by Kansas City, Missouri toward effective finance personnel management. The focus of the article is on the reasons for using interns in municipal government, how to recruit qualified interns, and the procedures for conducting an intern program.

3. County and Municipal Clerks

Cape, William H., and Scruggs, B. L. "In-Service Training Aids City and County Clerks," *Kansas Government Journal,* XLIX (January, 1963), 12-14.

This article gives a general background on the reasons why orientation for public service is necessary and desirable. It also gives information on types of assistance available for Kansas city and county clerks and describes three-day in-service training schools at the University of Kansas and the subjects discussed. It urges that leaders in city and county government be utilized to help in-service training.

City Clerk's School: A Report. Lawrence: Governmental Research Center, University of Kansas, Annual.

An annual function since 1953, the City Clerk's School is a short in-service training course dealing with major functions and problems of municipal administration. The Reports consist of the various lectures and discussions.

Compilation and Digest: 1961 Municipal Clerks and Finance Officers Institute. Sante Fe: Municipal League of New Mexico, May 31, 1961, 46 pp.

This compilation and digest consists of summaries, outlines, or complete talks prepared by the program participants. It does not include material discussed during the question and answer periods.

County Clerks School: A Report. Lawrence: Governmental Research Center, University of Kansas, Annual.

Includes presentations made at the School and notes taken by members of the staff. The School attempts to aid in improvement of the professional ability of the clerks and provide them with the opportunity to learn more about their administrative problems. Recognized leaders in the field of county government and related areas assist in programming and instruction.

Fourth Annual Work Shop Conference of City Clerks and Finance Officers Division, September 15, 17, *1958, Springfield, Missouri.* Springfield: Missouri Department of Finance, October, 1958, 32 pp.

This publication includes addresses on "Duties of a City Clerk," "Financial Reports Records," and "Initial Steps in Setting Up of Zoning Regulations." Each address is followed by a panel discussion.

Goldrick, M. D. "The Training and Development of Senior Administrators in Canadian Municipal Government," *Canadian Public Administration,* VI (June, 1963), 156-220.

In the section relating to development of professional standards are descriptions of training programs for clerks and treasurers arranged by province. This is preceded by a detailed description of local government in Canada and its officials, particularly clerks and treasurers. Included also are the responses to a questionnaire about the same officials.

Institute for Colorado Municipal Clerks and Finance Officers, . . . Proceedings. Boulder: Bureau of Continuation Education, Department of Political Science, University of Colorado, Annual.

A summary of presentations made at the Institute including the more informative questions and answers.

Lawton, John W., and others. *A Working Guide for Training in Records Management.* Washington, D.C.: Communications Resources Division, United States Agency for International Development, 1963, 130 pp.

Designed for use by instructors, the Guide includes suggestions on setting up a training course, conducting it, a detailed outline of the course, and suggestions for the instructor and for workshop projects.

The Office of Town Clerk. Albany: The Association of Towns of the State of New York, 1960, 107 pp.

Prepared by the staff of the Association as part of its program of education and in-service training of town officers, this manual discusses the duties of town clerks and contains a statutory index.

Papers Presented at Training School for Fiscal Officers and Municipal Clerks of Cities and Villages. Albany: New York State Department of Audit and Control, Annual.

Contains the papers relative to municipal finance in New York State presented at the annual school sponsored by the Conference of Mayors and Other Municipal Officials of the State of New York, New York State Society of Municipal Finance Officers, and New York State Association of City and Village Clerks in cooperation with the New York State Department of Audit and Control.

Proceedings of the First Annual Conference for Municipal Clerks. New Brunswick: Bureau of Government Research, Rutgers University, August, 1959, 30 pp.

The contents cover "State-Wide Legal Development Affecting Municipalities," "Ordinance, Resolution, and Motion Procedure and Minute-Taking," "Filing and Indexing of Municipal Records," and "Personal Records Management."

Proceedings of the School for County Commissioners: A Collection of Addresses Presented at the Training School for County Commissioners and Chief Clerks.

Harrisburg: Pennsylvania Department of Internal Affairs, 1964, 62 pp.

This school was held "to acquaint new commissioners with the nature of their duties and to disseminate new information to those who previously held office."

A Report of the . . . Annual County Clerks School. Lawrence: Governmental Research Center, University of Kansas, Annual.

A report of a session of a program for leaders in the field of county and local government designed to provide new ideas and methods of management for both new and experienced clerks.

School for Town Clerks. Albany: Town and County Officers Training School of the State of New York, 1966, 4 pp.

This pamphlet contains the program of the School for Town Clerks held at Cornell University, July 11-13, 1966 and sponsored by the Town and County Officers Training School of the State of New York.

C. Fire Protection

1. Surveys, Descriptions, and Analyses of Local Training Needs, Resources, and Programs

Adley, Stephen P. "Confidence in Their Ability, Knowledge Of What To Do, and Courage To Do It Constitute the Fundamentals of Pittsburgh's Fireman Recruit Training," *American City,* LXXVI (September, 1961), 161, 163.

Discussed here are the program, organization, and content of the three-week training program required of Pittsburgh Fire Department recruits.

"The Annual Pennsylvania Fire School: Firemen Are Trained in All Aspects of Fire Fighting at School in Lewistown," *Municipal Administration* (March, 1952), 3-4.

The annual fire school, conducted by Public Service Institute of Pennsylvania, is one feature of a year-round fire training program, including local classes held without expense to local communities. The fire school is offered to local communities in Pennsylvania and other states and consists of about thirty hours of instruction in five days.

Annual Report: California Fire Training Program. Sacramento: California Department of Education.

A report of the year's accomplishments in the State Program of Fire Training covering the work performed by the program supervisor and eight travelling instructors of fire training.

Annual Training Report. Albany: Division of Fire Safety, New York State Office for Local Government, Annual.

This annual report contains descriptive material concerning courses taught in the standard state fire training program. Ten courses are offered by the Division of Fire Safety to the fire service and are entitled: "Essentials of Firemanship," "Fire Investigation," "Fire Inspection Practices," "Ladder Company Operations," "Officer Training," "Pump Operator," "Single Company Operations," "Radiation Safety for Firemen," "Aircraft Fire and Rescue," and "Fire-Police Course." The courses are taught by part-time instructors, and workbooks for students in these courses are prepared, published, and distributed by the Division of Fire Safety.

Barnett, W. H. "State Coordinated Fire Department Training," *Florida Municipal Record,* XXXIV (May, 1960), 5-6.

The various services Florida's Fire College provides the many fire departments throughout the State are discussed in this article.

Beliveau, Roger, Gascon, Jacques, and Barrette, Rogation. *Duties and Responsibilities.* Montreal: Montreal Fire Department, January, 1966, 175 pp. (Mimeographed.)

A basic training manual for the Montreal Fire Department in both English and French. It shows many European methods of fire fighting not usually employed in the United States.

"Cincinnati Fire College Provides Broad Training for City's Fire Fighters," *Fire Engineering,* CXV (September, 1962), 780-83, 855-56.

New recruits to Cincinnati's fire department receive training for ninety eight-hour days at the well-equipped Cincinnati Fire College. Also, the regular companies report to the fire college twice yearly for instruction and/or examination.

Dekter, Cliff. "Fire Department Recruits Go To College in California," *Fire Engineering,* CXIX (December, 1966), 45.

This article reports on a cooperative program in which Pasadena City College conducted a fire service basic training course for recruits of the fire departments of twenty cities in northern and eastern Los Angeles County.

————. "Los Angeles County Keeps Training Program Up To Date," *Fire Engineering,* CXVIII (March, 1965), 34-35 and 65.

Surveyed briefly here are some of the more interesting aspects of the training programs of the Los Angeles County Fire Department.

Fire Department Instructors Conference. Chicago: Western Actuarial Bureau, 1967, 238 pp.

The proceedings of the fire department instructors conferences, co-sponsored by the Memphis Fire Department and the Western Actuarial Bureau, are in journal form and are records of the conferences held in Memphis, Tennessee. Held annually, they generally deal with fire training methods, applications, and techniques.

"Fire Department Training Facilities," *Firemen,* XXVIII (March, 1961), 9-11.

This article contains information about and pictures of municipal training centers obtained from a survey of cities of 25,000 or more population.

"Firemen's Training in the Months Ahead," *Firemen,* XXXIII (June, 1966), 27.

This article lists alphabetically by state and Canadian province training courses being offered, their dates, and name and address of person to whom to write for information.

Fire Training Program, Annual Fire School. Olympia: State Board for Vocational Education, June, 1961, 110 pp (Mimeographed.)

The proceedings of the annual training school held in the State of Washington.

Fuchs, Frank H., and Silvern, Leonard C. *Training Firemen Using An Aural-Visual Teaching Machine.* Los Angeles: Education and Training Research Laboratories, Hughes Aircraft Company, 1962, 21 pp.

Administration and results of an evaluation study of an experiment in using teaching machines to teach firemen a lesson on "Fire Behavior."

Hanifin, Frank. "How New York Improved In-Service Training: A Survey, Six Months Later, Reveals Greater Efficiency," *Fire Engineering,* CXV (February, 1962), 120-22.

The key to New York's success in improving its in-service training program was to improve the quality of instruction with a course designed to teach instructors the most effective methods of on-the-job instruction.

Hanna, R. E. (ed.). *Proceedings for Fire School.* Morgantown: University of West Virginia, 1966, 267 pp. (Mimeographed.)

The proceedings of the annual training school held in the State of West Virginia.

Hilliker, Floyd. "Cross-Training Police and Firemen," *Mayor and Manager,* IX (February, 1966) 24-25.

The cross-training and cooperative program between the police and fire departments in East Grand Rapids, Michigan are described.

Improving Fire Equipment Operation Through Firemen Training: Michigan Fire Department Training Program. Lansing: Michigan Board of Control for Vocational Education, 1944, 20 pp.

Information on the various kinds of training programs and the possible financial assistance available to local Michigan fire departments.

Jacobsen, Adolph P. "Training Center for a Small Department," *Firemen,* XXX (June, 1963), 18.

The author describes the Bloomfield, Connecticut training building for firemen.

Just, J. W. *Survey of Training in the Fire Department of the City of New York.* New York: Office of the Mayor, March-April, 1951, 14 pp.

A highly critical report of the program at the time the survey was made. Within this report, "A Suggested New Training Program," presents recommendations intended for the New York City system, but also suggestive for other departments. "A Comparative Training Outline of Other Departments" presents pertinent information for nine other large cities.

Management Survey of the Fire Training Program, Department of Education, State of California. Sacramento: Organization and Cost Control Division, California Department of Finance, December 19, 1958, 8 pp.

This survey is the result of a legislative analyst's recommendation that funds for the state fire training programs be disallowed. The State of California Department of Education conducts training programs for local districts, employing full-time itinerant instructors who present courses on the basis of the local need. This system is described and reasons for retaining it in essentially the same form are presented.

McCraw, Guy L. "Joint Training Effort Utilizes Instruction, Practice at Grand Prairie's Modern Plant," *Texas Town and City,* XLVII (November, 1960), 15.

A report is made in this article on a one-day, fire-fighting training session which offered three types of fires for practice—burning autos, smokey oil pit, and the fourth floor of a practice tower.

Municipal Fire Administration. Chicago: International City Managers' Association, 1956, 442 pp.

A four-page discussion of training for firemen and officers, with brief mention of specific programs in various localities, is included in the chapter on Personnel Management.

Municipal Fire Defense Institute: A Service of the American Municipal Association. Washington, D. C.: Municipal Fire Defense Institute, American Municipal Association, 1961, 7 pp.

A description of the history of the Institute, its policy, organization, program, and membership information.

"New York's Training Program," *Fire Engineering,* CXV (December, 1962), 1120-021.

A survey of the basic training program conducted by New York City's Fire Department training center on Welfare Island.

Nolting, Orin F. "Group Training in Fire Department Administration," *Firemen,* XIX (December, 1952), 16.

This article describes and gives examples of the use of the manual, "Municipal Fire Administration," prepared by the Institute for Training in Municipal Administration.

O'Brien, Donald M. "Training Fire Department Rescue Personnel," *Fire Engineering,* CIX (August, 1958), 710-713, 784.

This article is a general study of various efforts being made to intensify and broaden fire department training programs to meet increased demands on fire rescue and emergency forces.

Presentation of Additional Training Opportunity to Evanston Police and Fire Departments. Evanston: City Manager's Office, 1958, 7 pp.

This was an announcement by the City Manager of a nineteen week course of training designed to make better police officers and help them understand how they can assist fire companies in emergencies.

Proceedings of the . . . Annual West Virginia Fire School. Morgantown: Department of Mining and Industrial Extension, University of West Virginia, Annual.

Some of the addresses given at the school are provided in the proceedings. The amount of material printed varies from year to year, but the more advanced subjects are usually covered.

Proceedings of the Symposium on Higher Education for the Fire Service, Albany: Division of Fire Safety, New York State Office for Local Government, February, 1967, 300 pp. (Mimeographed.)

Proceedings of a meeting held by fire service and educational leaders to determine what courses of action should be followed in developing college courses and programs for both the paid and volunteer firemen.

Report of . . . Annual Arizona State Firemen's College. Phoenix: Arizona Department of Vocational Education, Annual.

Unedited manuscripts of the reports presented at the annual college which is "an organized attempt to acquaint firemen with some of the newer ideas, methods, and equipment used in the complex science of the fire service."

Report of the Session of the Tennessee State Fire Service School. Nashville: Tennessee Board of Vocational Education, 1965, 54 pp.

A report which includes the principal addresses made and a description of the demonstrations at the session.

Rescue Training Course. Hartford: Connecticut Office of Civil Defense, April, 1952, 129 pp. (Mimeographed.)

This is a textbook-workbook of rescue techniques for a course offered to firemen and civil defense workers.

Rogers, James C. "Training Center in Nassau County," *Firemen,* XXIX (August, 1962), 16-17.

A description of the training center in this New York State county, its buildings, and its equipment. The article includes a sketch of the layout and a list of tips for planners of training facilities.

"School for Fire District Officers," *Fire District Topics,* XX (June, 1965), 1-4.

Contains the program of the School for Fire District Officers held at Cornell University, Ithaca, New York on June 28-30, 1965 and conducted by the Town and County Officers Training School of the State of New York.

Scott, C. L. "Training a Municipal Fire Department," *Firemen,* XIX (December, 1952), 12-13.

This article includes reasons for the need for well-trained fire departments, components of a successful training program, and a description of the Memphis, Tennessee program.

Selected Papers Presented at the . . . Annual Fire Department Instructors Conference. New York: International Association of Fire Chiefs, Annual.

The papers were chosen on the basis of being most appropriate for the membership of the International Association of Fire Chiefs.

A Selection of Papers Presented at . . . Annual Seminar and Training Course in Arson Detection and Investigation, Purdue University, Lafayette, Indiana . . . 1950-1954. New York: International Association of Fire Chiefs, Annual.

The seminar is a "review of the problem of arson with emphasis on the latest techniques and methods of detecting, apprehending and prosecuting the arsonist."

Silvern, Leonard C. "Implications of Teaching Machines for Fire Service Training," *Fire Engineering,* CXIV (April, 1961), 290-91, 307-09.

This article describes how teaching machine lesson plans were prepared for a Los Angeles County Fire Department training program. It discusses the principles, strengths, and limitations of programmed instruction.

————. *A Progress Report on the Development of a Lesson in "Fire Behavior" for the Los Angeles County Fire Department.* New York: International Association of Fire Chiefs, 1961, 6 pp.

This report, an address given at the Eighty-Eighth Conference of the International Association of Fire Chiefs, includes the discussion which took place after the speech.

"Survey of State and Provincial Firemen's Training, 1959," *Firemen,* XXVI (November, 1959), 20-25, 36-37.

The primary purpose of this article was to indicate some of the trends and new items of interest. Reports, arranged alphabetically by state or province, cover state-wide training programs and not classes conducted on a local or area level. There is a short summary at the beginning of the article. This survey has been made annually and reported in succeeding years of this publication.

Temby, L. E. *Instructional Television Report Presented at the Annual Conference of the League of California Cities, Fire Chiefs Department.* Berkeley: San Bernardino Valley College, October 12, 1965, 6 pp.

Because of the lack of qualified instructors and long distances to be covered in the area, San Bernardino Valley College instituted a firemen's training course on educational channel television. Advantages and disadvantages, with suggested solutions to problems, are presented. College credit is given upon completion of the course.

"Training in Principal Fire Departments," *Firemen,* XXXII (December, 1965), 17-18.

A questionnaire, prepared by the National Fire Protection Association Fire Service Directory, was sent to fire chiefs of communities over 20,000. It asked various questions about their current training facilities and programs.

Training Manual. La Habra, California: La Habra Fire Department, 1964, 138 pp.

Instructions in the manual establish a coordinated policy for fire fighter training and standardize the methods and procedure in fire department training and drill evolution for La Habra.

Training Manual and Duty Manual. Wichita: Wichita Fire Department, 1966.

These manuals summarize the firefighting knowledge and training the recruit firefighter must secure.

Virginia State Fire School, Norfolk, Virginia, September 9-13, 1957. Richmond: Fire Chiefs Association, 1957, 96 pp.

This publication covers presentations by specialists in the various phases of firemanship—some at general sessions, some at group discussions. Topics in the latter include: teaching methods, structural fires, fire department rescue, salvage, ladders, fire pumps, and several other problems.

Whale, Malcolm D. "Public Service Training Available to Cities and Villages," *Michigan Municipal Review,* XXV (February, 1952), 23-24.

A brief description of the Michigan Town Fire School Program and the additional training services for firemen conducted by the State.

Winger, Robert M. "The Michigan Town Fire School Assists Small and Volunteer Departments," *Michigan Municipal Review,* XXIII (March, 1950), 43.

The Michigan Town Fire School Training Programs are conducted by visiting instructors who utilize the equipment and facilities of the community where the class is held.

2. General References on Purpose, Development, Organization, and Evaluation of Training Programs

Auxiliary Firemen: Suggested Training Manual. Austin: Texas Division of Defense and Disaster Relief, 1954, 110 pp.

Includes information for the use of the instructor and auxiliary firemen in training programs as well as outlines for each class session of a suggested training program.

Bond, Horatio, and Kimball, Warren Y. *Industrial Fire Brigades Training Manual.* Boston: National Fire Protection Association, 1954, 158 pp.

Practices outlined in this manual were compiled to reflect the recommendations made by insurance inspection departments, central managements, and public authorities.

Civil Defense and Disaster Relief Training Manual for Auxiliary Firemen, Basic Course. Sacramento: California Department of Education, 1951, 118 pp.

Material prepared from the outline developed by chief officers and training directors in a series of conferences held in California. With the exception of the first chapter, "Overview of Civil Defense," the manual is similar to that for regular firemen. It deals with technical information about fires and firefighting equipment.

Douglas, R. J., and Hediburg, R. *The Fire Department Officer.* Norman: University of Oklahoma, 1960, 67 pp.

Used for in-service training in twenty-seven states, this manual discusses the fire fighting and non-fire fighting activities of all fire officers and correlates the entire fire department organization. It also deals with decisions, planning, activating, problem solving, delegating responsibilities, and supervision.

Fire Control: Flammable Liquids and Gases; California Fire Training Program. Sacramento: California Bureau of Industrial Education, 1964, 241 pp.

This publication shows how to set up practice fires with small, inexpensive props, outlines practice drills step by step, presents demonstrations for the drill field and classroom, and contains related information and sources of visual aids.

Fire Control Simulator. Ames: Fire Service Extension, Iowa State University, 1966, 14 pp.

A discussion of the design of a fire situation simulating device that can be used in the training of officers.

Fire Department Training Manual. Phoenix: Fire Department, 1956, 141 pp.

A manual which covers basic operations in the handling of hose lines, ladders, and equipment.

Fire Prevention Training Course. College Station: Texas Firemen's Training School, Engineering Extension Service, Texas Agricultural and Mechanical College System, no date, 70 pp. (Mimeographed.)

This text material describes how to structure and maintain effective fire prevention programs for communities.

"Fire Training by Machine: A Los Angeles County Experiment," *Fire Engineering,* CXIV (January, 1961), 32-33.

This is a description of a teaching machine, how it is used, the lesson plan, and possible future experiments.

Fire Training Manual: Book One. Atlanta: Atlanta Fire Department, 1965, 142 pp.

A guide for daily operations and an aid for continued improvement and education. Twenty-one chapters are on various aspects of fire fighting.

Fire Training Program, Fire and Arson Investigations. Olympia: State Board for Vocational Education, 1961, 60 pp. (Mimeographed.)

A lesson plan on Penal Law arson investigation and fire department responsibility in dealing with the cause of arson.

Fuchs, Frank H., and Silvern, Leonard C. *Training Firemen Using An Aural-Visual Teaching Machine.* Los Angeles: Education and Training Research Laboratories, Hughes Aircraft Company, 1962, 21 pp.

Administration and results of an evaluation study of an experiment in using teaching machines to teach firemen a lesson on "Fire Behavior."

Glines, David F. *What a Fireman Should Know About Arson.* Sacramento: Bureau of Industrial Education, California State Department of Education, 1961, 141 pp. (Mimeographed.)

A text manual prepared to give firemen a basic understanding of the Penal Law, methods of arson investigation, and personality types that are frequently involved in arson incidents.

Granito, Anthony R. "Programmed Instruction in Ladder Training," *Fire Engineering,* CXXI (February, 1968).

Describes the program learning techniques used in teaching recruit firemen the use of fire ground ladders. It includes concepts developed in training firemen.

Guide to the State Fire Training Program, rev. ed. Albany: New York State Division of Safety, 1954, 116 pp.

Description of the program including how to initiate, plan, and conduct the training in a local program, certification of graduates, and the public relations aspect.

Hose Manual. Fresno: Fresno Fire Department, no date, 70 pp.

This manual provides a detailed description and instructions for operation of various kinds of fire hose.

Hudiburg, Everett. *Fire Service Practices for Volunteer Fire Departments.* Stillwater: Department of Fire Protection Technology, Oklahoma State University, 1958, 113 pp.

A manual developed to present those training practices most nearly consistent with the activities of smaller fire departments. It includes practices with respect to forcible entry, portable fire extinguishers, salvage and overhaul, fire apparatus, ventilation, rescue, and rope, ladder, and hose practices.

Lesson Plans: Fire Training Program. Albany: New York State Bureau of Fire Mobilization and Control, no date, 311 pp.

Consists of three courses: basic, intermediate, and advanced. The courses begin with the elements of firemanship and progress to more advanced phases of work. The lesson plans included give complete instructions for preparing, teaching, and testing a lesson.

Lesson Plans: Single Company Operations: Graduate Fire Training Program. Albany: New York State Bureau of Fire Mobilization and Control, 1954, 83 pp.

Designed to develop training teams or companies, the plans are complete instructions for preparing, teaching, and testing a lesson.

Manual in Basic Fireman Training for Volunteer Firemen. Salt Lake City: Utah State Board for Vocational Education, 1961, 270 pp. (Mimeographed.)

This manual is a series of volumes and includes all areas of fire training for volunteer firemen. It also presents workbook material that can be utilized by instructors.

Manuals and Texts in Fire Service Training. Stillwater: Fire Protection Department, Oklahoma State University, no date, 14 pp.

These manuals and texts cover the following topics: "Fire Service Training;" "Instructors and Drill Masters, Company Officers;" "Related Informal Texts;" "Special Job Training;" "Fire Chiefs and Chief Officers;" and "Basic Science and Mathematics."

Methods of Instruction and Establishing a Training Program. Albany: Division of Fire Safety, New York State Office for Local Government, June, 1967, 38 pp. (Mimeographed.)

A lesson plan developed for instructing departmental training officers in the theory of learning, teaching methods, and structuring of training programs to meet departmental needs.

Mueniter, Otis. *Auxiliary Firemen: A Suggested Training Manual.* Austin: Texas Division of Defense and Disaster Relief, 1959, 122 pp.

The purpose of this manual is to furnish information for the use of both the instructor and the auxiliary fireman in the advancement of training programs in the twelve disaster districts of Texas. It is directed to improving already existing training programs and to provide guidelines for the further development of such programs.

Nolting, Orin F. "Group Training in Fire Department Administration," *Firemen,* XIX (December, 1952), 16.

This article describes and gives examples of the use of the manual, "Municipal Fire Administration," prepared by the Institute for Training in Municipal Administration.

Proceedings of the Symposium on Higher Education for the Fire Service. Albany: Division of Fire Safety, New York State Office for Local Government, February, 1967, 300 pp. (Mimeographed.)

Proceedings of a meeting held by fire service and educational leaders to determine what courses of action should be followed in developing college courses and programs for both the paid and volunteer firemen.

Radiation Hazards in the Fire Service. Portland: Training Bureau, Portland Fire Department, no date, 81 pp. (Mimeographed.)

Problems encountered by firemen at radiation incidents are discussed as well as the techniques for eliminating problems of this nature, especially in transportation accidents.

Rafferty, Max. *Fire Control: Flammable Liquids and Gases.* Sacramento: Bureau of Industrial Education, California State Department of Education, 1964, 241 pp. (Mimeographed.)

A text manual to give firemen basic training in the safe handling of volatile liquids.

The Red Book Series. Stillwater: Department of Fire Protection Technology of the Technical Institute, College of Engineering, Oklahoma State University, various dates.

Training manuals have been issued in the *Red Book* series. Discussed in the manuals are the types of equipment used, training methods in teaching the use of equipment, and application of the equipment at fires. The titles of the manuals include: *Hose Practices in Fire Service Training* (1961); *State Firemanship Training Programs* (1962); *Ventilation Practices in Fire Service Training* (1959); *Water Supplies for the Fire Service* (1964); *Mathematics Applied to the Fire Service* (1954); *Rescue Practices; Salvage and Overhaul Practices* (1956); *Fire Apparatus Practices* (1942); and *Fire Apparatus Practices* (1953).

A Reference List for Firemen's Training. Boston: National Fire Protection Association, 1948, 19 pp.

A selected list of titles prepared to assist instructors and members of firemen's basic or elementary training classes.

Training Firemen to Make Dwelling Inspections. Boston: National Fire Protection Association, 1964, 24 pp.

This was not intended to cover the entire field of planning and conducting home inspections but rather those phases which are the responsibility of the training staff. It includes an outline and bibliography.

Training Manual. La Habra, California: La Habra Fire Department, 1964, 138 pp.

Instructions in the manual establish a coordinated policy for fire fighter training and standardize the methods and procedure in fire department training and drill evolution for La Habra.

Training Manual and Duty Manual. Wichita: Wichita Fire Department, 1966.

These manuals summarize the firefighting knowledge and training the recruit firefighter must secure.

Virginia State Fire School, Norfolk, Virginia, September 9-13, 1957. Richmond: Fire Chiefs Association, 1957, 96 pp.

This publication covers presentations by specialists in the various phases of firemanship—some at general sessions, some at group discussions. Topics in the latter include: teaching methods, structural fires, fire department rescue, salvage, ladders, fire pumps, and several other problems.

Whale, Malcolm D. "Public Service Training Available to Cities and Villages," *Michigan Municipal Review,*

XXV (February, 1952), 23-24.

A brief description of the Michigan Town Fire School Program and the additional training services for firemen conducted by the State.

Winger, Robert M. "The Michigan Town Fire School Assists Small and Volunteer Departments," *Michigan Municipal Review,* XXIII (March, 1950), 43.

The Michigan Town Fire School Training Programs are conducted by visiting instructors who utilize the equipment and facilities of the community where the class is held.

D. Health

1. Public Health Functions in General

Amos, Franklyn B. "The Public Health Training Program of New York State," *Public Health Reports,* LXVIII (March, 1953), 295-300.

The historical and political background of New York State's public health training programs and some details regarding organization, budgeting, and qualifications required of trainees are covered in this article.

Amos, Franklyn B., and Morgan, Annie W. "Training for Medicare Responsibilities," *Public Health Reports,* LXXXI (October, 1966), 870-74.

The organization and curriculum of a series of five-day orientation courses on hospital procedure are covered in this article. The courses—sponsored by the New York State Department of Health with the cooperation of the Columbia University School of Public Health and Administrative Medicine—were designed to help health department personnel meet their new responsibilities under the Medicare legislation.

Anderson, Otis L. "Training Opportunities for Public Health Personnel," *Public Health Reports,* LXXII (August, 1957), 681-86.

The author discusses the need for more and better qualified personnel, the kind of training required, and the financing of such training programs. The Public Health Service traineeship program is also described.

Awards to Individuals: Public Health Traineeship Program, rev. ed. Washington, D. C.: United States Public Health Service, 1963.

A description of the policies and procedures pertaining to the traineeship for graduate or specialized public health training.

Baumgartner, Leona. "A Personnel Education Program in the Department of Health," *American Journal of Public Health,* XXX (February, 1940), 119-28.

This report, by the Director of the relatively extensive in-service training program conducted by New York City's Department of Health, covers objectives, fellowships and scholarships, intra-mural courses, travel, fellowship, teaching centers, staff meetings, and a table of specific in-service training courses.

Blackerby, Philip E., Jr. "Field Training for Public Health Dentists," *American Journal of Public Health,* XLV (January, 1955), 28-32.

The author recommends the development of appropriate field training programs as an integral part of the graduate education of the public health dentist.

Culbert, Robert W. and others. "Training Programs in School Health Service," *American Journal of Public Health,* XLIV (February, 1954), 228-34.

This article covers instructional and training programs in theory and practice of school health service, elementary and secondary, for the student teacher, the medical student, the newly employed school physician, and the graduate public health student.

A Guide to Special Administrative and Managerial Training Programs. Washington, D.C.: Personnel Management Branch, Employee Development Section, United States National Institute of Health, 1962, 32 pp.

This guide lists courses available throughout the country, arranged by subject with information as to place, data, description, qualifications, and tuition.

Hofheinz, Roy. "Houston's Goal—First-Aid Training for Every City Employee," *American City,* LXX (January, 1955), 113-14.

The author explains the role he played and the approach he took, as Mayor of Houston, to encourage the participation of city employees in a combined civil defense and first aid training program.

Homemaker Service Training Syllabus. Elko, Nevada: Visiting Homemakers Service of Northeastern Nevada.

The Service, a pilot project under the United States Public Health Service, developed the syllabus to provide the instructor-coordinator with materials to construct the individual training session in each area of the multi-county district.

Lehman, S. P., and Peterson, D. R. "Public Health Residency Training," *Public Health Reports,* LXXII (May, 1957), 436-40.

The primary emphasis of this report concerns various aspects—curriculum, organization, etc.—of the residency training program in public health service conducted by the Seattle-King County Department of Health.

Malcolm, James C. "Experiences in Orientation of New Staff," *California's Health,* XI (May 15, 1954), 177-79.

Discusses some of the more important points relative to a three-day field trip program offered to new staff members after they have been with the Alameda County Health Department for approximately three months. The program is directed at developing a team spirit by giving an overview of the jobs of other members of the department.

Mason, Karl M. "The Public Health Training Program in Pennsylvania," *Public Health Reports,* LXIX (April, 1954), 372-74.

Article gives the background for the State's training program and describes the types of training offered through the Field Training Center at Pittsburgh.

Merritt, E. G. "Employee Training As a Full-Time Staff Function," *Hospitals* (September 1, 1960), 30-33.

A well planned training program can improve hospital patient care, employee morale, and public relations.

New York State IHHC Management Institute: Summary of Proceedings, June 17-19, 1962. Albany: New York State Department of Civil Service, 1962.

Contains a summary report of the addresses given and the discussion of various groups in the Institute which was organized and directed by the New York State Department of Civil Service in cooperation with the New York State Interdepartmental Health and Hospital Council, and held at State University College, New Paltz, New York.

O'Brien, Henry R. "Training of State and Local Health Workers in a Southern Region," *American Journal of Public Health,* XLII (October, 1952), 1223-231.

The article gives examples of training programs in Region III of the United States Public Health Service—North Carolina, Virginia, Maryland, West Virginia, Baltimore, and District of Columbia—for public health nurses, health officers, laboratory workers, sanitarians, and personnel of tuberculosis and other hospitals. Charts and maps are included.

————. "Why and How State Health Departments Organize for Training: Patterns and Trends," *Public Health Reports,* LXX (April, 1955), 393-401.

The current status of public health service training is revealed by a nation-wide study conducted by the United States Department of Health, Education and Welfare.

Phillips, Charles W. "Job Development and Training for Workers in Health Services," *Health, Education, and Welfare Indicators* (August, 1966), 14-26.

Background summary of the plan and program of a three-day conference on the subject and highlights of the conclusions reached.

Ritvo, Miriam M., and Oram, Phyllis G. "Meeting Resistance to Change in an In-Service Training Program," *Adult Leadership,* IX (November, 1960), 146-48, 164.

The authors describe an in-service human relations workshop sponsored by the Newton-Wellesley Hospital in Newton Lower Falls, Massachusetts and discuss many factors that played a part in making the employees enthusiastic for the program.

The Role and Training of Professional Personnel in the Field of Aging. Washington, D.C.: United States White House Conference on Aging, April, 1961, 58 pp.

"A statement of needs, approaches, and programs, together with recommendations." Topics covered include roles for professional personnel, approaches to professional training, and current activity in education and training. The primary emphasis is on university training.

Schaefer, Norman C., and Soller, Genevieve R. *Training Nursing Home Aides: A Descriptive Report of a Pilot Study in Oklahoma, January 1 - December 31, 1958: A Cooperative Study Conducted by the Department of Health, State of Oklahoma and the United States Public Health Service.* Oklahoma City: Oklahoma Department of Health, 1959.

The pilot study was undertaken to promote the manual "How To Be A Nursing Aide in a Nursing Home," and to test its effectiveness. The report includes the method of procedure, the data collected, and an appendix containing sample forms.

Soller, Genevieve R. "Training Nursing Home Aides," *Public Health Reports.* LXXV (April, 1960), 283-90.

The author recapitulates the highlights of the method, findings, and recommendations of a pilot study financed by the United States Public Health Service to test their manual, *How To Be A Nursing Aide in a Nursing Home.*

Spiegel, Allen D., and others. "Evaluating Short Health Training Courses Through Content Analysis," *Public Health Reports,* LXX (January, 1955), 75-80.

The authors evaluate a study conducted by the Bureau of Public Health Education of the New York City Department of Health. The study used content analysis to judge the effectiveness of an in-service training program for dental hygienists.

Traineeship Grants for Short-Term Training Under the Public Health Traineeship Program. Washington, D.C.: United States Public Health Service, 1962.

This provides information concerning application procedures and prescribes the terms and conditions governing the grants made to public or non-profit institutions which will conduct the short term training programs.

Underwood, Bruce, and others. "Courses for Nursing Home Personnel," *Public Health Reports,* LXXIV (November, 1959), 985-1000.

Under the above title, three separate articles deal with the problem of providing adequate training for nursing home personnel. Each offers a slightly different view of the problem and suggests different programs.

Van Buren, James K., and Prior, Margaret M. "In-Service Training in Stroke Rehabilitation for Care Facility Personnel in Oregon," *Public Health Reports,* LXXIX (January, 1964), 73-76.

A report on a brief training program (two classes of three hours each) for nursing home employees, plus a discussion on why efforts to make a critical evaluation of the program were unsuccessful.

Weiss, Robert L., and others. "Retreading Public Health Workers Through Training," *American Journal of Public Health,* LV (February, 1965), 242-67.

Organized somewhat like a symposium, this article presents a series of papers that deal with the problem of updating health personnel in such fields as dental health, public health nutrition, mental health, health education, and laboratory personnel.

2. Environmental Health

Bender, Maurice. "The Clean Air Act and Its Implications for Training Requisite Personnel," *Journal of the Air Pollution Control Association,* (December, 1965), 573-75.

Describes why the passage of the Act made it necessary to find the most effective way to train additional administrators and staff for work in air pollution control agencies, and covers the recommendations of the special meeting of the Surgeon General's Air Pollution Committee and thirty consultants on how the training should be accomplished.

Brumbaugh, Lester R., and Dunphy, Howard. "In-Service Training as Conducted by the San Joaquin Mosquito Abatement District," *California Vector Views,* V (July, 1958), 43-46.

The purposes of the in-service training program are to inform the employees of new materials and techniques, equipment, and insecticides, to create awareness of the characteristics which distinguish one type of mosquito from another, to review agency objectives and the reasons policy decisions are made, and to increase staff identification with the program of the agency.

Carson, Adrian L., Jr. "An In-Service Training Program for Sanitarians in Virginia," *Public Health Reports,* LXXVI (January, 1961), 83-84.

Virginia's in-service training program for sanitarians originally was forced upon it as virtually the only answer to a serious situation. The program has been of such obvious value to both the public and the State Department of Health that current plans are to strengthen it even though the emergency is definitely over.

Environmental Health Survey Report and Recommendations. Cincinnati: Robert A. Taft Sanitary Engineering Center, United States Public Health Service, 1963-64.

This is a four-part survey report of an environmental health survey by the Public Health Service. The report was made during the presentation of a training course on Urban Planning for Environmental Health which was conducted by the California Department of Public Health and the Public Health Service and co-sponsored by the League of California Cities. The four parts, each dealing with a California municipality and its adjacent area, follow in general the same format: a section on program implementation; individual reports such as water services, housing, and planning; a profile of the area; and a summary of recommendations.

"Environmental Health Training Program, 1964-65," *Public Health Reports,* LXXIX (May, 1964), 457-58.

A list of short term training courses offered by the Public Health Service during the fiscal year 1965 through the Training Program of the Robert A. Taft Sanitary Engineering Center in Cincinnati, Ohio. Courses include training in radiological health, air pollution, water supply and pollution control, food protection, metropolitan planning, and occupational health.

Environmental Sciences and Engineering Training Program Bulletin of Courses, July 1964 - June 1965. Cincinnati: Robert A. Taft Engineering Center, United States Public Health Service, 1964, 62 pp.

This covers technical and orientation courses, training institutes, and technical seminars for scientists, engineers, and other professional people in the fields of radiological health, air pollution, water supply and pollution control, food protection, metropolitan planning, and occupational health.

O'Brien, Joseph F., and Amos, Franklin B. "New York State Training Program for Sanitation Personnel," *Modern Sanitation,* IX (April, 1952), 17-21, 71.

Findings, opinions, and recommendations of a committee appointed to analyze the educational and training needs of sanitation personnel employed in the State.

Training Course, Environmental Health Survey Report, and Recommendations, St. Joseph County, Indiana. Cincinnati: Robert A. Taft Sanitary Engineering Center, United States Public Health Service, 1964, 79 pp.

This survey was conducted as a training exercise during the course on Urban Planning for Environmental Health, June 15-20, 1964. The report includes a section on program implementation, and sections on individual group reports such as water services, housing, planning, and other topics.

Training Course, Environmental Health Survey Report, and Recommendations, Wayne Township, New Jersey. Cincinnati: Robert A. Taft Sanitary Engineering Center, United States Public Health Service, 1964, 66 pp.

This survey was conducted as a training exercise during the course on Urban Planning for Environmental Health, June 2-4, and 9-11, 1964. The report includes a section on program implementation, and sections on individual group reports such as water services, housing, planning, and other topics.

Weston, Conley W. "Training New Sanitarians in Virginia," *Public Health Reports,* LXXII (August, 1957), 750-52.

Discusses the program adopted in Virginia to improve the quality of sanitation services, reduce the turnover of sanitarians, and increase the effectiveness of the recruitment of trainees. The major points covered are training and more equitable salaries.

3. Mental Health

Belkin, Marvin, and others. "Mental Health Training Program for the Child Health Conference," *American Journal of Public Health,* LV (July, 1965), 1046-056.

The report evaluates the effectiveness of an in-service training program for physicians and nurses which was aimed at teaching the application of mental health concepts in day-to-day duties.

Cape, William H. *Seminar for Directors of Mental Health Centers: A Report.* Lawrence: Governmental Research Center, University of Kansas, October, 1962.

This seminar provided an opportunity to discuss administrative problems. The subjects ranged from social psychiatry to public relations. The report includes addresses made and the small group discussion of problem cases.

Ferry, Charlotte. "An Experiment in In-Service Mental Health Education for Public Health Nurses," *California's Health,* XVII (November 15, 1959), 97-100.

A report of the educational aspect of public health nursing experience in the development of a mental health program in Contra Costa County, California. Under this program, public health nurses are assigned to a patient needing intensive mental health care prior to the patient's release from the county hospital psychiatric ward. The nurse works with the patient in the home environment following his release.

Gundry, C. H., and others. "An In-Service Training Project in Mental Hygiene: How Can A Social Worker Assist Public-Health Nurses in a Mental-Hygiene Program?" *Mental Hygiene* (January, 1953), 47-60.

The authors discuss reasons for adding a social worker to

the staff, and describe various methods used in Vancouver by the social worker to help the nurses work more effectively in the area of mental hygiene.

Parker, Beulah. "The Nature of Mental Health Teaching In A California Public Health Department," *California's Health,* IX (January 31, 1952), 105-09.

A carefully planned educational program for nurses and others who work with children is the subject of this study. It discusses why the program failed and how it was successfully changed.

Parnicky, Joseph J., and Ziegler, Richard C. *In-service Training for Attendants in Institutions for the Mentally Retarded: A Survey and Framework.* Trenton: Division of Mental Retardation, New Jersey Department of Institutions and Agencies.

This report on a three-phase project to develop a curriculum guide for attendant training includes a survey of institutions, based on a questionnaire, in-service training, and a workshop for developing a framework for the guide.

E. Libraries

Bassam, Bertha, and others. "Training for Technical Services," *Library Resources & Technical Services,* VIII (Winter, 1964), 35-46.

Representatives of academic and public libraries and library schools discuss the type and amount of training needed in library schools and on the job for librarians in technical services departments of libraries.

Bowler, Roberta. (ed.) *Local Public Library Administration.* Chicago: International City Managers' Association, 1964, 375 pp.

This guide for chief administrators and governing bodies of cities and counties on the best policies and programs provides the librarian, library staff, and library trustees with an appreciation of important library concerns and sets forth accepted administrative methods for getting library work done.

―――――. "Staff Development," *Local Public Library Administration.* Chicago: International City Managers' Association, 1964, 165-69.

A report discussing the need for outlines and kinds of programs available for in-service training and continuing education.

"In-Service Training," *Wilson Library Bulletin,* (April, 1950), 596-607.

Four papers presented at a forum on the subject are covered. The contents are: "Training the Staff to Understand Library Policies," "Training the Staff in Processes," "Training the Staff for Professional Participation," and "Training the Staff in Community Participation." The Foreword includes five recommendations that came out of the discussion following the presentation.

Shank, Russell. "In-Service Training in Libraries," *American Library Association Bulletin,* LV (January, 1961), 38-41.

A preliminary report on in-service training trends as reported by libraries to the ALA Library Administration Division, Personnel Administration Section's In-service Training Committee.

Sheil, Marion D. "Cuyahoga County Library Tackles the Recruitment Problem in a Practical Way, With Its Newly-Developed Intern Program," *Library Journal,* LXXX (June 1, 1962), 2093-095.

The plan described combines study in a nearby school of library science with work in the library in a specific professional position whereby the student can obtain his Master's Degree in Library Science in three years.

Stallmann, Esther L. *Library Internships: History, Purpose and a Proposal.* Urbana: Library School, University of Illinois, January, 1954, 23 pp.

This discussion falls into five parts: (1) internships in the development of library education, (2) internship as a form of education used by other professions, (3) the need for library internships, (4) major problems, and (5) a proposal for library internships.

Walker, H. Thomas. "In-Service Training for Subprofessionals," *American Library Association Bulletin,* L (February, 1956), 134-38.

This article deals with a Maryland Division of Library Extension program, responsibility for which is shared by the participating libraries. Program content is given as well as schedule of classes. The author describes the type of student participation and some of the problems, and discusses attempts at evaluation.

Wilson, Celianna I. "Professional Internship: A Program and a Proposal," *Library Journal,* LXXXI (June 1, 1963), 2201-005.

The author, Personnel Librarian at the Ohio State University Library, describes its first internship program and proposes for libraries an internship program modeled after that of the medical profession.

F. Planning, Housing, and Community Development

Arend, Frederick H., and others. "Many Pathways Opening Up For Careers in Housing and Community Development," *Journal of Housing,* XXII (February, 1965), 74-91.

Under this general title, the authors have written on the following topics: "HHFA Washington Intern Conference Demonstrates Scope of Community Development Career," "New York City Intern Program Is Bringing Trained Young People Into Big City Renewal," "Corinth Trainee Program Introduces Young People to Small City Renewal," "In-Service Training Through Federal-State Aid Looked to As a Career Builder," "Public Housing Design Seminars Opening Up New Vistas For Housing Officials, Architects," and "Management Training Institutes for Public Housing for Elderly Evolving New Job Concept."

Brennan, James J. "Needed: Effective Training for Municipal Progress," *B.O.C.A. News,* (August, 1963), 3-6.

The author of this article in the publication of the Building Officials Conference of America urges preparation of a master plan of education for the professionalization of the building inspection service and makes specific suggestions as to how this can be accomplished. He also recommends a national council of the professional associations of government workers which would concern itself with professional development of the public service in general.

Brignac, Robert. "New Orleans Authority Maintenance Men Go To School," *Journal of Housing,* XVI (February, 1959), 62-65.

In an effort to cut costs, the Housing Authority of New Orleans surveyed its maintenance men, decided training was necessary, and set up a course in building maintenance with the cooperation of the State-supported vocational and technical school.

"Chicago's In-Service Training Program," *Building Standards Monthly* (August, 1955), 7-9.

Reviews the history and activities of the Advisory Committee on In-Service Training for Chicago's Building Department, and evaluates the in-service training program. Recommendations for future training activities are presented.

Colling, R. C., and Colling, Hal, eds., *A Training Manual in Field Inspection of Buildings and Structures.* Los Angeles: International Conference of Building Officials, 1956, 174 pp.

This was planned as a teaching syllabus for instructors in university courses but developed into an outline text for the courses and a supplemental guide to inspection techniques.

The Eighth Series of Graduate Fellowship Awards for City Planning and Urban Renewal. Chicago: City Planning Fellowship Program, Sears-Roebuck Foundation, 1963.

A brochure giving information on how and where to apply for an award, who is eligible, where the studying is to be done, and the kinds of grants.

Federal-State Training and Research Programs for Community Development: An Information Bulletin. Washington, D.C.: United States Housing and Home Finance Agency, 1965, 5 pp.

This covers the main features of Title VIII of the Housing Act of 1964, the plan a state must design to be eligible for a matching grant, and the training and research programs eligible for assistance.

Frith, G. E. "Training in Housing Management," *Housing* (June, 1951), 18-21

Training schemes in two large British housing authorities are described as well as the author's suggestions as to allocation of time spent in practical training, his advice to students, discussion of financial assistance to students, and the need for staffs to obtain wider experience in the general work of the department.

Housing Management Training: A Committee Reports Activity to Date and Recommends a Program. Chicago: Management Division. National Association of Housing Officials, August, 1941, 31 pp.

A report based on forty replies to a detailed questionnaire. It begins with a brief survey of training efforts and proceeds with an analysis of two kinds of management training schemes—short and long term programs. The former are considered in detail and specific recommendations are made. Problems inherent in the latter are indicated.

Hunter, Donald F. "In-Service Training Adds Enthusiasm, Competence to Housing Code Inspection Job," *Journal of Housing,* XI (February, 1954), 51-52.

The author describes recruitment, training plan, method, and follow-up training. He outlines the course, session by session, and the one-week refresher course.

"In-Service Training Feature of Local, Federal, Business Organizations," *Journal of Housing,* XIII (August-September, 1956), 282-83.

This article deals with the plans and programs for in-service training of various housing agencies and organizations—Chicago Housing Authority, San Antonio Housing Authority, Housing and Home Finance Agency, National Association of Real Estate Boards, Savings and Loan League, and Pacific Coast Building Officials Conference.

Institute on Community Planning and Development. Des Moines: Iowa Development Commission, September, 1964.

This publication covers a series of workshops programmed to provide detailed information and procedures in the administration and utilization of comprehensive planning in government. It includes instructor's outlines, addresses given, a bibliography, and sample forms. The topics covered included planning, zoning, subdividing, and legislation.

Jenkins, Bette. "Detroit Housing Commission Has In-Service Training For All Employees," *Journal of Housing,* XIII (August-September, 1956), 277-78, 283, 288.

The author describes how the Detroit Housing Commission went about developing a training program that would reach all employees and give them an insight not only into their own specific jobs but into the overall housing and renewal program. The results of the program after two experimental years are summarized.

Leathers, Carl R., and McKee, Franklin D. "The View from the Bottom Rung," and "A Junior Planner Catches On." *Tennessee Planner,* XXI (March, 1962), 92-95.

Two graduates of an intensive ten-week training course in planning given by the Tennessee State Planning Commission express their reactions to the course.

"London Holds First School for Housing Staffs," *Public Service,* January, 1956, 12-13.

Describes a weekend school on housing for professional or technical examination students.

"Maintenance Clinics: First 'Shirtsleeve' Sessions a Success; Program Catching On," *Journal of Housing,* XII (May, 1955), 160-61.

These clinics were sponsored jointly by the Technical and Maintenance Section of the National Association of Housing and Redevelopment Officials and the Public Housing Administration. The article includes information on where the clinics were held, who attended, and what industries participated. Detailed information about the "Model Clinic" in Washington, D. C. is also given.

Matson, J. Warren. "Train Managers to Play Public Relations Role in Community," *Journal of Housing,* VII (April, 1950), 137.

This article describes a series of conferences between the management staff of the Pittsburgh Housing Authority and representatives of agencies involved in the redevelopment of the City.

McLean, Mary, ed. *Local Planning Administration*. Chicago: International City Managers' Association, 1959, 467 pp.

This publication sets forth basic principles of community planning, provides practical suggestions for carrying principals into effect, emphasizes methods and procedures to provide a day-to-day working manual, and brings up to date changes that have taken place in the field.

Nash, Peter H., and Shurtleff, James F. "The Case of the Case Study in City Planning and Municipal Management," *Journal of the American Institute of Planners*, XXII (Summer, 1956), 153-72.

The role of the case study both as a tool of research and as a training device for budding practitioners of urban planning and city management is analyzed.

Petrie, Harry P., Dolbeare, Louis P., and Shaffer, Paul E. *Meeting the Recruitment Crisis, Planning 1957: Selected Papers From the National Planning Conference, San Francisco, California, March 17-21, 1957*. Chicago: American Society of Planning Officials, October, 1957, 237-52.

A paper giving suggestions for meeting the recruitment problem by improving organization and personnel administration generally, including the training program. It describes a Los Angeles County program for selecting senior or graduate students in appropriate fields of study for work full time during the summer and half time during the school year. Students are rotated through various sections and given close supervision and training by section heads. A second program employs similar students on a work assignment basis without rotation and with less formal training.

The Pittsburgh Plate Glass Foundation Announces A Fellowship Program for Graduate Study in City Planning and in Urban Renewal and Redevelopment. Pittsburgh: Graduate School of Public and International Affairs, University of Pittsburgh, 1962, 2 pp.

An outline of the terms governing the awarding of the grants, how they can be used, and the procedure to be followed in applying for awards.

The Pittsburgh Plate Glass Foundation: Program of Grants in Support of Urban Studies, Architecture and Community Development. Pittsburgh: Pittsburgh Plate Glass Foundation, 1963, 22 pp.

Discusses the need for training people in these fields, announces new programs in urban studies, reviews continuing grants of the Foundation in all three fields, and reports on the Foundation's cooperation with community development agencies.

"A Planning Education Report." *Journal of the American Institute of Planners*, XXIV (1958), 28-32.

Recommended in this report is an "action program" which would survey members for information on training programs.

Proceedings . . . Annual Institute for Planning Officials. Boulder: Bureau of Governmental Research and Service, University of Colorado, Annual.

The *Proceedings* cover various topics in planning such as fundamentals in planning and the role of the planning board.

"Renewal Training—LPAs Gain from Plan Mapped Out by URA, NAHRO," *Journal of Housing*, XVIII (January, 1961), 23.

Covers the background and some major rules and regulations for the Local Planning Authorities Trainee Program, a cooperative effort of the Urban Renewal Administration and the Renewal Division of the National Association of Housing and Redevelopment Officials.

Schatz, Donald, "The New York City Housing Authority Police: A Specialized Force," *FBI Law Enforcement Bulletin*, XXXV (November, 1966), 12-16.

A brief study of the New York City Housing Authority Police Force covering its history, organization, and operation. This special force has its own police training center. In size, the force ranks twenty-fourth in the nation.

Shirt Sleeve Clinics: A Guide for the Conduct of a Work-Shop Training Program for Housing Authority Personnel. New York: New York Regional Office, United States Public Housing Administration, 1957, 26 pp.

The experience of the New York Regional Office of the Public Housing Administration in conducting a series of maintenance training conferences in 1955 and 1956 forms the basis for this guide intended for use by others conducting similar training programs.

Shirt Sleeve Maintenance Clinic . . . Newark: New Jersey Housing Authority, June 15, 1959, 14 pp.

The purpose of this clinic was to discuss and demonstrate the ways and means by which maintenance costs can be reduced through greater efficiency in operations, and to permit discussion, exchange of experiences, and performance of corrective maintenance.

"Short-Course Training in City Planning: Report of the Committee . . .," *City Planning in the South*. Atlanta: Southern Regional Education Board, January, 1954, 123-28.

The purpose of the Committee was to consider how best to meet the need for formal training courses of short duration in the field of city planning. Issues considered included which groups should be reached, who should conduct the training, and what types of training should be undertaken.

Smigielski, W. K. "The Training of Planners," *Journal of the Town Planning Institute*, XL (June, 1954), 162-65.

This article extracts material from a paper read to the North of England Division of the Town Planning Institute on December 8, 1953. It refers to requisite qualifications for a planner, his basic education, and the use of models.

"Staff Training—It Takes New Techniques to Get Good Results," *Journal of Housing*, X (August-September, 1953), 272-73.

This article summarizes and quotes from an article by Charles S. Weber of the Michigan Civil Service Commission entitled "Getting Results from Training," in the May, 1953 issue of *State Government*. It includes a list of what Mr. Weber considers the fundamentals in setting up an employee training program.

Summary of Proceedings: Short Course for County Zoning Administrators. Tallahassee: Bureau of Governmental Research and Service, Florida State University, 1959, 55 pp.

This course covered how to start a county zoning program,

how to determine land use, what to include in zoning regulations, principles of administration, duties and responsibilities of zoning directors, effects of a limited access highway, and reasons for having county zoning.

Training Conferences, April 16-20 and June 4-6, 1956. Washington, D. C.: United States Housing and Home Finance Agency, 1956, 278 pp.

This covers the text of presentations made at the conferences which were part of a series of efforts to bring about effective coordination of programs administered by the Agency and its constituents. References are made to various visual materials that were used but these are not reproduced. Included are various special glossaries and a bibliography.

A Training Program for Housing Management: Learning from Practical Experience. Chicago: Management Division, National Association of Housing Officials, March, 1941, 22 pp.

This publication covers general information, suggestions to supervisors, and suggestions to trainees.

"Training to Be a Housing Manager: A Model Training Scheme Prepared by the Institute of Housing and Circulated to All Local Authorities in England. Wales and Scotland," *Housing* (March, 1960), 119-21.

General advice on how and where the Training Scheme should be used plus a detailed outline of its three parts.

G. Police

1. General

a. *Surveys, Descriptions, and Analyses of Local Training Needs, Resources, and Programs*

Allen, Edward J. "Upgrading the Uniformed Patrolman," *California Peace Officer,* XIV (May-June, 1964), 5, 49.

The rotation system used by the Santa Ana Police Department to broaden the experience of its men in uniform is discussed, together with the problems created by the system, and the changes made.

Annual Report. Chicago: Training Division, Police Department, Annual.

This report covers a summary of the various basic programs and special programs by statistical table and written report.

Anslinger, H. J. "Narcotics Bureau Conducts Training School for Police," *FBI Law Enforcement Bulletin* (October, 1962), 7-10.

The author discusses the origin of the school, diversity of the students, what is taught, how it is taught, and teaching personnel.

Bancroft, Raymond L. "Municipal Law Enforcement 1966," *Nation's Cities,* IV (February, 1966), 15-26.

A survey which was conducted by the National League of Cities covering both recruit training and in-service training of police departments. Only three per cent of the surveyed agencies reported no recruit training. In the field of specialized training programs, eighty-one per cent reported that they conducted their own police training courses.

Two appendices indicate the scope of work and professional examination for a housing manager.

"Unique Instruction for City Planners: Institute Course in Planning Methods and Techniques Assists Specialists in New Field," *Popular Government,* XXVII (March, 1961), 8-9.

In the intensive two-week course in city planning methods and techniques held at The Institute of Government, University of North Carolina, a substantial part of the one hundred hours of instruction was spent on field surveys and practical planning design problems.

Winston, Oliver C. "Training . . . for Baltimore's New Employees," *Journal of Housing,* VIII (January, 1951), 21-23.

Describes the four-session orientation program for new employees of the Housing Authority and the reasons for its importance.

Zimmerman, Joseph F. "A College Seminar for Planning Board Members," *American City,* LXXIV (August, 1958), 24.

Describes the first seminar of its kind for members of Massachusetts town planning boards designed to give them an overview of the planning process and assistance with specific problems.

Blatt, Genevieve. "From the Pennsylvania Department of Internal Affairs: Police Training—A Program for Pennsylvania," *Pennsylvania Chiefs of Police Association Bulletin,* XXVII (Winter, 1966), 10, 24.

A review of proposed state legislation creating a Municipal Police Officers' Standards and Training Commission in the context of what other states are doing and what it would mean to Pennsylvania policemen.

Boolsen, Frank M., and Peper, John P. *Law Enforcement Training in California.* Sacramento: Bureau of Industrial Education, California Department of Education, 1959, 174 pp.

A publication containing factual material on various types of training and educational programs and the practices and procedures involved.

Brandstatter, A. F. "Law Enforcement Training in Michigan Provides Opportunities for Municipalities." *Michigan Municipal Review,* XXIV (February, 1951), 27, 34.

The author highlights the purposes and objectives of police training and discusses the current and future plans of a state-wide training program in Michigan.

Brekken, James M., and Granger, Larry. "Bloomington Develops Comprehensive Police Training Program." *Minnesota Municipalities,* XLIX (July, 1964), 9-11.

An extensive analysis of the training program developed jointly by the Police Department and the Personnel Office in 1961. The article concentrates on the influence of learning ability, recruit training, in-service training, training bulletins, and the police library—all within the framework of the seven objectives of police training outlined in the beginning of the article.

Brereton, George H. "The Importance of Training and Education in the Professionalization of Law Enforcement," *Journal of Criminal Law, Criminology, and Police Science,* LII (May-June, 1961), 111-21.

The author discusses some of the highlights in the development of police education and training in the United States and singles out some of the individuals and organizations he feels have played an important role in this development.

Brown, William P., and others. "Training to Meet the Sex Criminal: Seminar," *Police Yearbook.* Washington, D. C.: International Association of Chiefs of Police, 1963, 157-65.

The reasons for training in this special field and the areas of police responsibility are listed here. Curricula of an FBI sex crime investigation school and morals squad course are presented.

California Peace Officer Standards Program. Sacramento: California Department of Justice, November, 1965.

This includes all the information needed by a city or county that wishes to participate in the program. It covers such things as steps necessary to take for participation, specifications for courses, where they can be taken, and the requirements for physical examinations.

Cape, William H. "Pursuing Basic Credentials in Law Enforcement," *Report of the Eighteenth Annual Officers Training School.* Lawrence: Governmental Research Center, University of Kansas, April 1, 1965, 1-8.

A description of the courses given at the school and evaluation of the school by the student officers are presented here. Professional characteristics of the officers and their comments on various aspects of the police job are included. The balance of this publication consists of lectures given as part of the training.

Carlin, Vincent A. "Police Executive Development Courses," *Police,* V (January-February, 1961), 62, 64-65.

A discussion of the procedure used by the New York City Police Department in developing police executives. It includes a discussion of background, procedure curriculum, and purposes of such courses.

Chapman, Samuel G. *Dogs in Police Work: A Summary of Experience in Great Britain and the United States.* Chicago: Public Administration Service, 1960, 101 pp.

Information concerning the training of dogs and handlers for the London Metropolitan Police as well as the organization and operation of a program in the United States.

Chisholm, John, and others. "Education and Training," *Police Yearbook.* Washington, D. C.: International Association of Chiefs of Police, 1954, 146-73.

Includes "Police Training" by John Chisholm; "The Psychological Training of Police Officers" by A. Canty; Improving Police Effectiveness by Education, Improved Promotional Methods, and Performance Evaluation" by A. F. Brandstatter.

Command Officers Training, December 3-7, 1951. East Lansing: Department of Police Administration, Michigan State College, 1951.

This publication covers the outlines of or the lectures presented at the five-day school. The subjects covered—one each day—were principles of leadership, administrative tools for leadership, principles of police administration and organization, supervisory techniques, and the police and the public.

"Committee Assists on In-Service Police Training," *Public Management,* XXXVII (September, 1955), 208-09.

Fifty-eight weekly one-hour courses covering thirty-eight subjects in police training were offered between October, 1952 and June, 1954 in Glendale, California. Attendance, which was voluntary, was quite high with eighty-five per cent of the employees attending over thirty per cent of the courses.

Culloo, Leo A. "Mandatory Police Training Law Effective July 1," *New Jersey Municipalities,* XLII (June, 1965), 18-19.

This article summarizes the Police Training Act of New Jersey, effective July 1, 1965, cites pertinent sections, explains some provisions, and lists locations of training schools.

————. "Police Training—An Investment in Community Security," *New Jersey Municipalities,* XLI (November, 1964), 55-56.

The author presents the argument backed up with figures that a new policeman represents such a large investment by a community that he should be trained. He also describes briefly the state-wide police training program.

————. "A Progress Report—The State-Wide Police Training Program," *New Jersey Municipalities,* XLIII (October, 1963), 25, 27.

A report covering the first year of operation of a state-wide police training program including location of facilities, number of officers enrolled, the curriculum, and other aspects.

————. "State Wide Police Training in New Jersey," *New Jersey Municipalities,* XXXIX (October, 1962), 5-6, 8.

The author argues for state-approved certification for all law enforcement officers in New Jersey and offers an outline of the proposed training program of the New Jersey Police Training Commission.

Denney, Jonathan F. "The Douglas Police Dog Training Program," *League of Arizona Cities and Towns Newsletter* (February, 1965), 1-2.

A short description of a police dog training program from the raising of funds to finance it, the volunteer work of building the facility, to the graduation ceremonies at the close of the first program.

Deppe, Donald A. "A Decade of Service to Law Enforcement Personnel: A Report on Education for Policemen at the University of Maryland," *Police,* IV (July-August, 1960), 68-71.

A report on education for policemen at the University of Maryland describing the Law Enforcement Institute, the Delinquency Control Institute, the Maryland Traffic Institute, the Police Professional Advancement Program, and the crime control curriculum.

Diamond, Harry. "Institute Planning," *Police Chief,* XXIX (January, 1962), 34-36.

Covers the planning, conducting, subject matter, and conclusions reached of the Institute on Arrest, Search, and Seizure conducted by the Department of Police Science and

Administration of the Los Angeles State College with the advice of various state, county, and local law enforcement agencies.

Ellis, J. T. "The Birmingham City Police Training Centre," *Traffic Digest & Review,* XIII (May, 1965), 10-14.

This article describes the physical facilities of the Birmingham, England Centre, its various courses, staff, and students, and how its objectives differ from those of other training programs.

Evans, David R. "Newark, Ohio Provides a Low-Cost Program for Police Training," *Ohio Cities and Villages,* XIII (September, 1965), 33.

The major points of how Newark, Ohio came to set up its own police training program, how it was organized, and the popularity it achieved are discussed.

"The FBI National Academy: Thirty Years of Progress Through Training," *FBI Law Enforcement Bulletin,* XXXIV (July, 1965), 2-6, 20-21.

A brief resume of the professional training program for law enforcement officers conducted by the FBI National Academy.

"FBI-PCPA Schools in Western Pennsylvania: Training Schools Conducted in the Boroughs of Indiana, Irwin, Somerset, Warren," *Pennsylvania Chiefs of Police Association Bulletin,* XX (Spring, 1959), 10-14.

This article gives short descriptions of training schools and law enforcement conferences in the area.

Fenn, G. E. "Training for Police Promotion Examinations," *Police Journal* (December, 1964), 582-88.

The author, head of the Durham County Constabulary, believes some sort of assistance is required to give candidates a reasonable chance of passing the English centralized promotion examinations. Consequently, he provides details of the training in police subjects given to his officers and indicates the means available to assist officers preparing for the education subjects.

Findlay, R. Dale. "Missouri Police Academy in Rolla Provides Law Enforcement Training," *Missouri Municipal Review,* XXX (May, 1965), 76-77.

Since the Missouri Police Academy was established by the state legislature in 1959, 2,041 local police officers representing 234 departments have received valuable tuition-free training in all phases of police methods. Courses are taught by the Missouri Highway Patrol and by instructors from the Northwestern University Traffic Institute. The school is "unprecedented by the fact that funds were allocated by the State" and there is no cost to the local municipalities.

Flanigan, John C. "How a Police Training Academy Was Established In a Small Department," *Pacific Northwest Law Enforcement News,* XXV (May-June, 1958), 34-39.

The Anchorage, Alaska Police Department established a training program for a force of about fifty officers. One officer was sent to the FBI National Academy and one to the University of Southern California. These two officers then acted as instructors for the program of basic training offered in two-week classes of eighty hours each. The content of the courses is outlined.

Fritz, Charles W. "It Couldn't Be Done!," *Police Chief,* XXVII (April, 1960), 30-32.

This is a description of the police training center of the small city of Norwood, Ohio.

Gallati, Robert R. J. "Some Modern Horizons in Police Training," *FBI Law Enforcement Bulletin,* XXVI (September, 1957), 7-9, 23.

The author, Commanding Officer of the New York City Police Academy, discusses the ideal training program for police officers and the steps taken by the New York City Police Academy to make such training available.

_____. "Where is 7 Hubert Street?," *Police,* IV (September-October, 1959), 19-25.

A concise outline of the training program of the New York City Police Academy located at 7 Hubert Street.

Gammage, Allen Z. *Police Training in the United States.* Springfield: Charles C. Thomas Publishers, 1963, 493 pp.

In-service police training, state-mandated and state-sponsored programs, and university and college training are covered in this book. A description of the major university programs, and a list of institutions conducting in-service training programs in 1962 is provided. Included is a directory of colleges and universities offering preparatory programs for careers in law enforcement and a bibliography.

Germann, A. C. "Modern Complex Police Duties Require Superior Personnel: Law Enforcement Education and Training in the United States," *Police Chief,* XXIV (October, 1957), 22, 24, 26, 28.

The author discusses what kind of training and education is required to produce the superior personnel necessary for discharging effectively the complex and demanding modern police tasks. He includes a section on academic and practitioner programs with tables of subject matter and institutions.

Gourley, G. D. "Incentive Higher Education Program for California Peace Officers," *California Peace Officer,* XII (March-April, 1962), 29-30.

A survey of the incentive technique in use in California cities.

Griffin, John I. "The Police Science Program," *Police,* V (November-December, 1959), 50-53.

Undergraduate and graduate programs for policemen are conducted by the Baruch School of City College of New York and the New York Police Academy where all students are law enforcement officers, and all instructors on professional subjects are New York City police officers.

Grothaus, Stanley R. "Compact Program Is Vital Phase of Police Training," *FBI Law Enforcement Bulletin,* XXXII (June, 1963), 15-19.

A report on three-day instructor course planned and conducted by the Cincinnati Division of Police for its supervisory personnel is reported on in this article.

Gruzanski, Charles V. "National Police Training Program Survey," *Police,* XI (September-October, 1966), 55-58.

This article gives the statistical results of a questionnaire dealing primarily with self-defense or physical training programs, which was sent to more than one hundred police departments in cities with populations of 85,000 or more.

Hankey, Richard O. "Training Through Teamwork," *California Peace Officer,* XI (March-April, 1961), 34-36.

"Teamwork and professional service" were the main themes of the first two homicide investigation institutes held at the Los Angeles State College of Applied Arts and Sciences. This report lists the cooperating organizations and the subjects covered.

Herman, Allen B., Jr. "The South Carolina Law Enforcement Training School (Division of General Studies and Extension, University of South Carolina)," *University of South Carolina Governmental Review,* (August, 1964), 1-4.

The coordinator of the South Carolina Law Enforcement Training School describes its origin, organization, and operation. A table gives the curriculum of the school.

Hess, Fred. "Police Training—Small Communities," *Journal of Criminal Law, Criminology, and Police Science,* XLIX (May-June, 1958), 75-77.

The author discusses the police academy of the Association of Chiefs of Police of Essex County, New Jersey, which provides a "Basic Police Course" for the police officers of the twenty-two member municipalities.

Hilliker, Floyd. "Cross-Training Police and Firemen," *Mayor and Manager,* IX (February, 1966), 24-25.

The cross-training and cooperative program between the police and fire departments in East Grand Rapids, Michigan are described.

Holmgren, R. Bruce. *Primary Police Functions.* New York: William C. Copp and Associates, 1960, 212 pp.

Covers the content of lectures and classroom sessions furnishing thirty-nine hours of formal instruction prepared originally as part of a training program for a ten-man police force of Lake Bluff, Illinois. It was first published as an in-service training series in *Law and Order* and includes three chapters on various aspects of public relations of police departments.

Holster, William. "Compulsory Training Required for Clifton Police," *New Jersey Municipalities,* XXXIV (November, 1957), 11-14.

The author, City Manager and Engineer of Clifton, New Jersey, presents a survey of the current training programs offered Clifton police personnel and outlines some additional programs which have been proposed and are under serious consideration.

Hoover, John Edgar. "The FBI National Academy," *Juvenile Court Judges Journal,* III (July, 1952), 4-7.

J. Edgar Hoover briefly reviews the history and organization of the FBI National Academy, which was established in 1935 to help train local police instructors and administrators.

In-Service Training in One-Man Car Procedure, December 14-18, 1953. Kansas City: Kansas City Police Department, 1953, 7 pp.

This covers simple instructions for officers with directions for instructors inserted at necessary points.

Intermediate Course for Police Officers. Albany: Municipal Police Training Council, New York State Office for Local Government, 1964, 10 pp.

An outline of the requirements of an Intermediate Course for police officers designed to provide all police officers throughout the State with an opportunity for continued instruction and study in the attitudes, knowledge, skills, and procedures involved in carrying out the duties and responsibilities of police work above and beyond the fundamentals covered in the basic training course.

Jelf, R. W. "Police College: The New 'A' Course," *Police Journal* (July, 1963), 326-33.

The commandant of Great Britain's Police College relates the changes to take place at that institution's course offerings, particularly the one preparing experienced sergeants for the responsibilities of the rank of inspector.

Johnson, Martin W. "Police Fleet Safety—Training and Disciplinary Practices," *Traffic Digest and Review,* XIII (August, 1965), 4-8; (September, 1965), 7-11; (November, 1965), 10-14.

These three articles are based on a research study by a 1964 graduate of the Northwestern University Traffic Institute. Part 1 covers the purpose of the study, and responsibility of administrative function of a departmental safety officer. It includes copies of the letter and questionnaire sent out; Part 2 covers current training practices; Part 3 discusses how awards and incentives can be helpful in reducing fleet accidents.

Johnson, William A. "Council to Standardize Police Training," *Michigan Municipal Review,* XXXVIII (May, 1966), 122-23.

This article describes the purpose, finances, and early work of the Council and its four committees. The Council was authorized by the 1965 Legislature.

Kassaoff, Norman C. "State Police Training Laws," *Police Chief,* XXXIII (August, 1966), 10-11.

A study of the various types of statewide police training legislation in the United States with particular emphasis on recent changes in Connecticut, Maryland, Illinois, Pennsylvania, and Louisiana.

Keuper, Vincent P. "Out of Urgency Grew the Monmouth County Police Academy," *New Jersey Municipalities,* XXXIX (June, 1962), 13, 15.

A New Jersey court ruling that a municipality can be held liable for negligence if it fails to give proper training to a municipal employee led to the establishment of the Monmouth County Police Academy.

Lee, A. J. "Brooklyn Center Initiates In-Service Police Training Program," *Minnesota Municipalities,* L (April, 1965), 11.

This program includes 180 hours of basic training, additional hours of specialized training; a cost-sharing plan—Village and Officer—for post-entry training; and seminars sponsored by Village and attended by surrounding municipalities.

Lewis, B. Earl. *A Study of Supervisory and Intermediate Retraining Needs in the Area of Law Enforcement Within the Foothill College District.* Los Altos Hills: Foothill College, February, 1965, 10 pp.

As a result of a new state requirement for supervisory training, a questionnaire was sent to the personnel of five local police agencies to determine interest in a proposed course. Tables show number and per cent of personnel interested, and preferences for type of training, subjects, time of offering, and method of offering.

Lindquist, John A. *Current Practices in Police Training.* Sacramento: Bureau of Industrial Education, Division of Instruction, California Department of Education, 1956, 36 pp.

A course outline prepared for use in connection with the California Peace Officers' Training Program at the Peace Officers' Administrative Institute, April 18 and November 8, 1956. It covers the need for training, history, programs of specific California cities, availability of specialized training, administrative problems of police training, organized self-training programs, and those offered by institutions of higher education.

Littlejohn, Frank N. "Training Program Development in a Police Department," *FBI Law Enforcement Bulletin,* XXVI (May, 1957), 13-15.

General material relating to the history and development of policies regarding police training activities in Charlotte, North Carolina, is presented in this article.

"Long Range Plan of Police Training Is Called A Success," *FBI Law Enforcement Bulletin,* XXX (April, 1961), 20-25.

A survey of the history of the development of training programs for law enforcement officers in New York State for the period 1945 to 1959.

MacNamara, Donal E. J. *A Study and Survey of Municipal Police Departments of the State of New Jersey.* Trenton: New Jersey Law Enforcement Council, May 6, 1958, 113 pp.

The chapter on Police Training discusses the prevailing situation in New Jersey, with emphasis on deficiencies, and a short legislative history. Recommendations include the text of a proposed act regulating standards and training suggestions for courses to be made available, and the establishment of a residential training facility.

McCandless, David A. "The Southern Police Institute," *State Government,* XXIV (August, 1951), 212-13 and 220.

A description of the program established at the University of Louisville's Southern Police Institute including its purpose, courses offered, nature of classes, names of nationally known specialists who have appeared there, and an evaluation of its effectiveness.

McGarvey, Francis S. "New York State Police Conduct Community Police Training," *Police Chief,* XXIII (March, 1956), 32-34.

A brief background report on the New York State School for Police—its purpose and normal operating rules and procedures, plus the early results of an experimental short training course given members of the Oswego Police Department.

Meehan, James B. "Police Participation in the College Training of Police," *Police,* VIII (March-April, 1964), 24-27.

The author discusses the relationship between the New York City Police Department and the Joint Police Science Program of the Baruch School of the City College of New York. Police Science courses are taught by professional police officers assigned to full-time duty at the school; other courses are taught by regular instructors. Degrees offered are B.B.A. in Police Science and Master of Public Administration with a major in police science.

The Michigan State University Police Administration Field Training Program As It Functions in Connec- *tion With Michigan State Government.* Lansing: Michigan Civil Service Commission, 1958, 13 pp.

Detailed description of the training which the Commission gives to senior students of the Police Administration School as part of their field service training program. Brief descriptions are given of the training in other state departments. Other governmental agencies and private industries participating in the training program are listed.

Morris, Willard B. "Minnesota's State Training Program for Local Law Enforcement," *State Government,* XXXIX (Autumn, 1966), 247-51.

Municipal police and sheriffs' departments may send officers to free regional training courses administered by the Police Training Division and its Advisory Board, and taught by instructors from police, government, and academic personnel.

Muehleisen, Gene S. "Standards and Training for Peace Officers," *FBI Law Enforcement Bulletin,* XXXIV (March, 1965), 11-15, 23.

This article discusses the history, organization, and goals of the California Commission on Peace Officer Standards and Training.

Municipal Police Administration. Chicago: International City Managers' Association, 1961, 545 pp.

Chapter five of this text, used for an in-service training course on police administration offered by the Institute, discusses post induction and pre-employment training that is available to police officers. The range of topics includes general considerations, basic recruit training, advanced in-service training, specialized in-service training, and training methods.

Municipal Police Training in New York State. Albany: Municipal Police Training Council, New York State Office for Local Government, 1961, 56 pp.

The Municipal Police Training Council Act was passed in 1959 creating a Municipal Police Training Council charged with preparing a mandatory municipal police training program. The Basic Training Course was developed by July 1, 1960 and all police officers, appointed after that date, are required to complete the course as a condition of permanent appointment. This publication is a detailed account of the first year of operation under this program.

Murphy, Patrick V. *In-Service Training Conference for Command Personnel: An Address.* Berkeley: Seminar on Police Planning and Research, University of California, 1958, 9 pp.

This is a discussion of training provided for all supervisory personnel in the New York City Police Department. The emphasis is on the principles of organization, supervision, administration, and personnel management.

————. *Police Administered Training in the United States.* New York: Police Academy Library, International Association of Chiefs of Police, 1965, 15 pp.

Covers data on training programs obtained as a result of questionnaires mailed to eighty police departments within four population groups, fifty state police agencies, and eight Canadian departments. It includes tables on such matters as the size of the instructional staff, recruit training, roll call training, refresher training, specialized training, and supervisory training.

Neyhart, Amos E. "Police Drivers Also Need Training," *Police Chief,* XX (January, 1953), 34-35, 37.

The case history shows how one police department made sharp cuts in its accident rates, costs, and time lost due to vehicle accidents by giving training courses in defensive driving to its drivers.

Nielsen, Judith. "The South Carolina Law Enforcement ETV (Educational Television) Training Program," *Traffic Digest and Review,* XIV (December, 1966), 3-6.

The South Carolina Educational Television Center—state-owned—cooperated with various groups to provide law enforcement instruction via closed-circuit television. The program has received a federal grant under the Law Enforcement Assistance Act of 1965.

Nimmo, George M. "Statewide Police Training for Sparsely Populated Areas," *FBI Law Enforcement Bulletin,* XXXIII (March, 1964), 12-16.

A brief study of the first six years of the Wyoming Law Enforcement Academy, the nature of the problems which led to its organization, and the current program offered.

O'Connor, George W., and Muehleisen, Gene S. "Mandatory Minimums or Professional Maximums, Training Seminar I," *Police Yearbook.* Washington, D. C.: International Association of Chiefs of Police, 1965, 307-17.

A discussion of the California POST program by Gene S. Muehleisen, Executive Officer of the program, with discussion and questions from the floor.

Owens, Robert G., and Hamann, Albert D. "Evaluating the Training Program," *Police Chief,* XXXIII(February, 1966), 22, 24.

To measure the effectiveness of its two-week institute "Delinquency Control for Law Enforcement Personnel," the Institute of Government Affairs tested the students both before and after the program. Sample questions are offered in the article.

"Peace Officers Training Council Created," *Ohio Cities and Villages,* XIII (August, 1965), 7-8.

The article gives the major provisions of the law creating the Ohio Peace Officers Training Council (Office of the Attorney General). The Council will consist of nine members appointed by the Governor with the advice and consent of the Senate and will have major powers and duties regarding police training in Ohio.

Peace Officer Training School. Lawrence: Governmental Research Center, University of Kansas, Annual.

In existence since 1947, the School helps officers keep up with new ideas and methods. The curriculum has changed as activities of officers have changed. The 1960 School had basic courses and special courses. The 1966 School held classes in Applied Police Science I and II and a three-day Correctional Officers Seminar. The reports are usually summaries of material presented at the School.

Peper, John P. "First Classes Held at New Riverside Peace Officers' Training Center," *Western City,* XXIX (June, 1953), 36, 59.

A history of the development leading to the creation of the Training Center at Riverside, California together with a discussion of how the program is run, sponsorship, and major problems in development and perspectives.

————. "Police Training in California," *Western City,* XXVI (September, 1950), 26-29.

A description of the California Program for Peace Officers' Training. The program is a pooling of experience, effort,

time, facilities, and money to provide training and training materials for the benefit of all California law enforcement officers. It covers both recruit and in-service training.

Police Officers' Pre-Promotional Training Program. New York: Police Academy, Port of New York Authority, no date, 145 pp.

This publication concerns itself with supervision and the functions of management as they both apply to the sergeant. It sets forth guide lines or principals for him to follow.

"Police Training: An Interview with Col. Anson B. Cook, Executive Director, Ohio Peace Officers Training Council," *Ohio Cities and Villages,* XIV, (August, 1966), 7-8.

An article covering the rules and regulations which the Ohio Peace Officers Training Council has the authority to recommend, and the answers to questions put to Mr. Cook in an effort to clarify the activities and requirements set by the Council.

"Police Training Officers Hold Conclave," *Police,* III (January-February, 1959), 73.

A brief report of the New York City Police Department ten day Institute for Police Training Officers.

"Police Training Program," *Public Management,* XLVI (April, 1964), 90.

A brief description of an extensive in-service training program in Washington Court House, Ohio, planned and coordinated by a sergeant who recently graduated from the FBI National Police Academy.

Presentation of Additional Training Opportunity to Evanston Police and Fire Departments. Evanston: City Manager's Office, 1958, 7 pp.

This was an announcement by the City Manager of a nineteen week course of training designed to make better police officers and help them understand how they can assist fire companies in emergencies.

President's Commission on Law Enforcement and Administration of Justice. *The Challenge of Crime in a Free Society.* Washington, D. C.: United States Government Printing Office, 1967, 340 pp.

A landmark report which may well provide the guidelines for future developments in the entire range of criminal justice activities, with specific recommendations on training.

President's Commission on Law Enforcement and Administration of Justice. *Task Force Report: The Police.* Washington, D. C.: United States Government Printing Office, 1967, 228 pp.

A document which presents a synthesis of the views of many prominent consultants and advisers in the field of police management and operations. Contains a model state act on training.

Proceedings, Seminar in Police Administration Conducted by the Center for Urban Studies in Cooperation With the Wichita Police Department, University of Wichita, July 23-24, 1959. Wichita: Center for Urban Studies, University of Wichita, 1959, 134 pp.

Tape recordings of the six panel discussions have been edited especially for this report.

"Professional Training at the Los Angeles County Sheriff's Academy," *California Peace Officer,* X (September-October, 1959), 6-7, 51-52.

A week-by-week description of the nine-week law enforcement training program of the Los Angeles County Sheriff's

Academy with comments on the typical reactions of recruits during each stage.

Progress Report, 1965. Sacramento: Commission on Peace Officer Standards and Training, California Department of Justice, April 1, 1966, 8 pp.

A report covering the first five years of this Commission which includes a summary of the law establishing the Commission and authorizing it to set standards and allocate funds to cities and counties from money deposited in the Peace Officer Training Fund from penalty assessments on fines collected for criminal offenses.

"Proposed Legislation: Federal Assistance to Law Enforcement," *Police Chief,* XXXII (August, 1965), 20-22.

This is the text of House of Representative's Bill, H. R. 6508, of March 18, 1965, to provide assistance in training State and local law enforcement officers followed by testimony of the Director of Professional Standards of the International Association of Chiefs of Police before a House Judiciary subcommittee hearing on the bill. Similar or identical bills are listed.

Ralston, Lee W. "Training the Teachers for Police Roll Call Training," *Journal of Criminal Law ,and Criminology,* XLI (September-October, 1950), 357-63.

The principles and methods followed for training supervising officers of the Los Angeles Police Department to plan and deliver brief training talks are covered in this article.

Report. Detroit: Detroit Citizens Advisory Committee on Police Procedures, March 22, 1960, 31 pp.

The focus of this report is on police training in community relations.

Richman, Grover, C., Jr. "Training Requirements for Local Police," *New Jersey Municipalities,* XXXII (February, 1955), 9-12.

The article discusses the current police training programs in New Jersey, recommends raising the job entry requirements of applicants, and suggests the adoption of the "police cadet plan" and on-the-job training.

Roberts, C. A. "How to Train a Motorcycle Squad," *American City,* LXXIX (February, 1964), 99.

The qualifications, recruitment, and classroom and cycle training of the specialized unit in Gainesville, Florida are covered.

"Rochester Plans College Course for Police Officers," *New York State Office for Local Government Newsletter,* V (May 30, 1966), 1, 3.

Covers a plan for training qualified high school graduates for appointment as police officers. It includes a two-year course at a community college, the State's basic training course, and part-time work in the Rochester Police Bureau.

Russell, C. W. "The Alabama Police Academy," *Alabama Municipal Journal,* XXIII (November, 1965), 15.

A description of the Alabama Police Academy which is conducted by the State for any law officer in Alabama without fees or tuition. The emphasis is on public relations and legal aspects of law enforcement.

Schatz, Donald, "The New York City Housing Authoritry Police: A Specialized Force," *FBI Law Enforcement Bulletin,* XXXV (November, 1966), 12-16.

A brief study of the New York City Housing Authority Police Force covering its history, organization, and operation. This special force has its own police training center. In size, the force ranks twenty-fourth in the nation.

Scheidt, Edward "Training School for North Carolina's Highway Safety Personnel," *State Government,* XXXI (April, 1958), 75-76, 80.

A description of how North Carolina's college-level driver training course for state highway troopers and license examiners came into being, the kinds of instruction it offers, and the encouraging gains that are coming from it.

Schroeder, Oliver, Jr. "Police Education: A University Aids the Smaller Departments," *Police,* V (November-December, 1959), 15-18.

A discussion of the police education program of the Law-Medicine Center at Western Reserve University in Cleveland. Basic concepts, curricula, and educational experiences are outlined.

Seale, Edwin L. "Orienting the Non-Examiner Police Investigators," *Police Chief,* XXIX (August, 1962), 24-29.

The author outlines and describes the training course in the utilization of the polygraph which he developed for criminal investigators of the Military District of Washington, D. C.

Siegle, Samuel. "Training Program for Morals Squad," *Police Chief,* XXVII (January, 1960), 16, 18.

A report and brief summary of topics covered at a twenty-eight-hour Morals Squad Course presented by the Federal Bureau of Investigation at the request of the Pennsylvania Chiefs of Police Association.

Sills, Arthur J. "The Mandatory Police Training Act in Quest of Uniform Minimum Standards," *New Jersey Municipalities,* XLII (October, 1965), 11-13.

The failure of voluntary police training programs in New Jersey and the growing complexity of the policeman's job made necessary the "Mandatory Police Training Act of 1965." This act set up the Police Training Commission which was charged with the responsibility of approving training schools, their administration, and curriculum. A chart of the thirteen schools in operation shows length of course, cost involved, time schedule, etc.

"Six Cities Organize Municipal Police Academy," *Public Management,* XLIV (May, 1962), 111.

Six suburban cities in the Dallas, Texas area formed the Dallas County Municipal Police Academy for in-service training and orientation. The academy is financed by the participating cities, and has an advisory board of two city managers and three police chiefs.

Snibbe, Richard H. "The Monterey Institute Program: A Unique Experiment in Advanced Police Training," *Police,* X (July-August, 1966), 95-96.

This article outlines the problems facing small police jurisdictions in providing advanced police training and the mechanics of an institute designed to resolve these problems including field processes, college processes, and combined field and college processes.

Southern Police Institute. Louisville: Southern Police Institute, University of Louisville, 1964.

A brochure describing the Institute which has two long terms of twelve weeks each in the Spring and Fall and four midwinter seminars, each two weeks long. Enrollment is limited to twenty-five specially-selected, higher-level law enforcement officers. It offers higher and more comprehensive training than is available within local departments.

State Crime Bureau and Police Academy: Report of the Colorado General Assembly. Denver: Colorado Legislative Council, December, 1961, 32 pp.

A report dealing with arguments for and against a proposed central crime bureau, and with training programs on law enforcement in Colorado. These include pre- and in-service training of the Colorado State Patrol, Denver Police Department pre-service recruit training, similar training in Colorado Springs and Pueblo, occasional short courses under Federal Bureau of Investigation auspices, and the annual crime institute in Boulder for all law officers. Increased training is proposed. Also given is information on law enforcement training in selected states—Pennsylvania, Ohio, Florida, and Kansas.

"State Police Training Program Attracts Over 600 'Students' in First Two Years of School," *Minnesota Municipalities,* XLVI (July, 1961), 211.

A brief description of the two week training schools for police officers held throughout the State of Minnesota between 1959 and 1961. The description includes a statistical report on attendance, a detailed delineation of the pattern followed, and a general evaluation.

"State Training Legislation," *Police Chief,* XXXII (August, 1965), 8-19.

An alphabetical list of states with summary digests of their laws or pending legislation providing for state-wide selection standards and state training programs for police.

"Statewide Police School Held in Washington State," *FBI Law Enforcement Bulletin,* XXVIII (October, 1959), 19-23.

A description of the origin of the Statewide Basic Law Enforcement Training School, its physical facilities, its courses of instruction, and the selection of its students. Similar descriptions of the Command School and the Fingerprint School are given.

Stottler, Richard H. and others. "Police Personnel," *Police Yearbook.* Washington, D. C.: International Association of Chiefs of Police, 1961, 168-98.

Partial contents are: "A Beginning Without an End" by R. H. Stottler; "Report of Education and Training Committee" by R. R. J. Gallati; "Advanced In-Service Training" by D. A. McCandless; "Role of the FBI in Police Training" by J. S. Rogers; "A Weakness in Police Training" by R. L. Holcomb; and "Need for Accelerated Progress in Training" by B. C. Brannon.

Sweeney, Faye B. "The Practical Patrolman School," *Law and Order,* (October, 1966), 8-9.

A description of a school for full and part time policemen from seven communities developed by the police chief of Belmont, New Hampshire (population, 2,500). The goal of the school is to give a student fundamental knowledge of his powers and duties and an opportunity to learn by participation in actual field problems.

Thomson, Louis M., Jr. "Toledo Police Academy," *Ohio Cities and Villages,* XIII (September, 1965), 30-31.

A brief history of the Toledo Police Academy and its accomplishments.

Training of Law Enforcement Officers in the Various States. Little Rock: Research Department, Arkansas Legislative Council, 1956, 21 pp.

A discussion of the information received from questionnaires circulated by other states in establishing programs for the training of law enforcement officers. The report focuses on the type, length, place, and costs of various programs as well as on the program operative in Arkansas at that time.

"Training Standards Sought in Florida and Ohio," *Police Chief,* XXXI (November, 1964), 44-45.

This article covers the appointment, purpose, and organization of the Florida Advisory Council for Law Enforcement Education and the draft of a bill to create the Ohio Law Enforcement Officers Standard and Training Commission.

Urquhart, Raymond M. "Mandatory Police Recruit Training," *Mayor and Manager,* III (November, 1960), 17-19.

The article deals with how the first state law requiring all police recruits to undergo a course of training was passed in New York, how it was put into motion, what types of courses are being given, what the course requirements are, and how community relations are stressed.

Van Asselt, Karl A. "Cooperative Training Program Assists Oregon Local Law Enforcement Officers, *Western City,* XLII (June, 1966), 34-35.

An outline of the general features of the program for advanced police training in fifteen regional schools in Oregon including locations of schools, subjects, sponsorship, and expansion of the program.

————. "Training Local Police Officers: A Field for State Leadership," *State Government,* XL (Autumn, 1967), 239-44.

The writer challenges the states to extend and accelerate their involvement and leadership in police training matters.

Waggoner, Hugh H. "State of Missouri Takes Step Forward in Police Training," *FBI Law Enforcement Bulletin,* XXX (February, 1961), 8-9.

The Missouri State Highway Patrol Academy at Rolla, Missouri was established by the Seventieth General Assembly of the Missouri Legislature which allocated funds to make police training available to all enforcement officers in the state.

Washington Needs Police Training: Report and Recommendations, 1961-1963. Olympia: Joint Committee on Governmental Cooperation, Washington State Legislature, 1963, 3-12.

A description of the Washington voluntary "basic schools" consisting of two-week courses precedes a discussion of the shortcomings of this system. The recommendation is for the establishing of a Washington law enforcement officers' commission to set minimum standards and provide reimbursement grants to local participating agencies. Funds would come from certain fines now allocated to the Current School fund.

Whisenand, Paul M. "Equipping Men for Professional Development in the Police Service: The Federal Law Enforcement Assistance Act of 1965," *Journal of Criminal Law, Criminology, and Police Science,* LVII (June, 1966), 223-27.

The author recommends that those responsible for police training—government training officials and University deans and faculties—need a re-analysis of what a police officer does and of the value of in-service training and university training.

Wilson, H. L. "In-Service Training on a Limited Budget," *California Peace Officer,* XII (May-June, 1962), 34-35.

The basic steps taken by members of the La Habra, California Police Department to plan, prepare, and produce a training program combining tape-recorded audio with 35 mm slide instruction are covered in this report.

Winkler, Frank J. "Law Enforcement Officer Training Program . . . An Opportunity for Cooperative Action," *Ohio Cities and Villages,* XI (October, 1963), 22-23.

Describes the Ohio Law Enforcement Officer Training Program, how and when a police chief may request assistance in training, and how communities can cooperate in using the training.

Wood, Allan C. "Basic Police Training in England," *Law and Order,* XIV (September 1957), 14-15, 56-57.

Description of the thirteen-week standard basic training, course by course, given to new recruits at the eight Police District Training Centres.

Wunsch, Edward F. "FBI-PCPA Intercounty Detective School," *Pennsylvania Chiefs of Police Association Bulletin,* XX (Spring, 1959), 2-5.

This article describes the School's curriculum and discusses the importance of this training.

York, Orrell A. "New York's Statewide Training Program for Municipal Police," *State Government,* XXXV (Winter, 1962), 30-33.

Police training, long considered a local function, is now being coordinated and certified at the state level in New York, following legislation in 1959 which resulted in the establishment of the first mandatory minimum training standards in the United States. Police officers, appointed after July 1, 1960, are required to complete an eighty-hour Basic Training Course satisfactorily as a condition of permanent appointment. Training schools are held on an area or local basis. Any police agency may sponsor a school if certified by the Council.

b. General References on Purpose, Development, Organization, and Evaluation of Training Programs

Aaron, Thomas J. "Considering a Training Program?" *Law and Order,* XIV (October, 1966), 14-15.

The author defines the three categories of law enforcement operations and the personnel responsibilities within the categories. He also advises on how to develop a good training program that reflects the differences in the categories and personnel skills.

Anderson, R. L. *Police Training in Criminal Procedure, Police Officers Training School, A Report.* Lawrence: Bureau of Governmental Research, University of Kansas, July, 1951, 49-55.

A suggested training program covering the crime of assault offered by Captain R. L. Anderson of the Police Training Division of Wichita, Kansas. The program is based on the trials and errors of experience and includes a detailed outline for each of the topics covered: criminal procedure, elements of the crime, assault investigation, and suggestions on courtroom testimony.

Answorth, Ray. "Are We Producing Police Administrators?" *Police Chief,* XXII (September, 1955), 14, 16, 18.

A discussion of three types of training programs: academic programs leading to degrees, specialized in-service training programs, and cadet programs.

Barnes, William M. "Tapping Community Resources for Police Training," *Police Chief,* XXXII (August, 1965), 42-46.

Helpful hints are given by the author on where to look within the community to find the organization with the facilities, training aids, and potential instructors for a proposed police training program.

Brown, William P., and others. "Training Implications —Planning and Research: Seminar," *Police Yearbook.* Washington, D. C.: International Association of Chiefs of Police, 1963, 150-57.

Members of the Saint Louis Police Department discuss in general terms the interaction between planning and training programs.

Chapman, Samuel G. *Dogs in Police Work: A Summary of Experience in Great Britain and the United States.* Chicago: Public Administration Service, 1960, 101 pp.

Information concerning the training of dogs and handlers for the London Metropolitan Police as well as the organization and operation of a program in the United States.

Chisholm, John, and others. "Education and Training," *Police Yearbook,* Washington, D. C.: International Association of Chiefs of Police, 1954, 146-73.

Includes "Police Training" by John Chisholm; "The Psychological Training of Police Officers" by A. Canty; "Improving Police Effectiveness by Education, Improved Promotional Methods, and Performance Evaluation" by A. F. Brandstatter.

Clift, Raymond E. "Police Training," *Annals,* CCXXCI (January, 1954), 113-18.

The author examines and appraises the training structure for policemen including pre-service, recruit, in-service, and on-the-job training as well as classroom training, and argues that training for the most part is geared to the top level while training for the "little fellow on the 'doing level' " remains the same.

————. "Police Training in the Smaller Communities," *Police Chief,* XXVI (September, 1959), 26-28.

The author suggests a number of guidelines he feels should be of use in determining who is likely to benefit most from a particular type of training course. Basically, he recommends a sharp differentiation between "refresher courses" and "basic theory courses."

Command Officers Training, December 3-7, 1951. East Lansing: Department of Police Administration, Michigan State College, 1951.

This publication covers the outlines or texts of the lectures presented at the five-day school. The subjects covered—one each day—were principals of leadership, administrative tools for leadership, principles of police administration and organization, supervisory techniques, and the police and the public.

Diamond, Harry. "Factors in Planning and Evaluating In-Service Training Programs," *Journal of Criminal Law, Criminology, and Police Science,* LIII (December, 1962), 503-06.

Two basic considerations of an in-service training program are the determination of training needs and the subsequent evaluation of the training effort. The author describes the Crawford Slip technique for spotting needs, and the aspects which, if measured accurately, might give an indication of the value of a recently completed program.

Germann, A. C. "Modern Complex Police Duties Require Superior Personnel: Law Enforcement Education and Training in the United States," *Police Chief,* XXIV (October, 1957), 22, 24, 26, 28.

The author discusses what kind of training and education is required to produce the superior personnel necessary for discharging effectively the complex and demanding modern police tasks. He includes a section on academic and practitioner programs with tables of subject matter and institutions.

————. "Police Training: Pre-Recruit to Retirement," *Quarterly Journal of the Association for Professional Law Enforcement* (October-December, 1959), 15-26.

The author reviews the possibilities of police training. He covers (1) pre-recruit: academic, cadet, and aide programs; and (2) in-service training: recruit, advanced or refresher, specialized, supervisory, and executive development.

Holmgren, R. Bruce. *Primary Police Functions.* New York: William C. Copp and Associates, 1960, 212 pp.

Covers the content of lectures and classroom sessions furnishing thirty-nine hours of formal instruction prepared originally as part of a training program for a ten-man police force of Lake Bluff, Illinois. It was first published as an in-service training series in *Law and Order* and includes three chapters on various aspects of public relations of police departments.

Howard, John P. "Integrating Public Relations Training For Police Officers," *Police,* VII (September-October, 1962), 57, 58.

Based on a concern for the maintenance of a good public image for municipal law enforcement, the author argues for the integration of public relations instruction with each subject taught in the training program rather than as a separate subject. Included is a discussion of what such an approach to public relations should cover and an illustration of how integration might be effected.

Intermediate Course for Police Officers. Albany: Municipal Police Training Council, New York State Office for Local Government, 1964, 10 pp.

An outline of the requirements of an Intermediate Course for police officers designed to provide all police officers throughout the State with an opportunity for continued instruction and study in the attitudes, knowledge, skills, and procedures involved in carrying out the duties and responsibilities of police work above and beyond the fundamentals covered in the basic training course.

Jameson, Samuel Haig. "Quest for Quality Training in Police Work," *Journal of Criminal Law, Criminology, and Police Science,* LVII (June, 1966), 210-15.

The author reviews police academy training and academic instruction and finds them inadequate for the needs of the modern police officer. He urges the adoption of a post-academy and post-academic program "geared to the tenents of current behavioral sciences."

Johnson, Martin W. "Police Fleet Safety—Training and Disciplinary Practices," *Traffic Digest and Review,* XIII (August, 1965), 4-8; (September, 1965), 7-11; (November, 1965), 10-14.

These three articles are based on a research study by a 1964 graduate of the Northwestern University Traffic Institute. Part 1 covers the purpose of the study, and responsibility of administrative function of a departmental safety officer. It includes copies of the letter and questionnaire sent out; Part 2 covers current training practices; Part 3 discusses how awards and incentives can be helpful in reducing fleet accidents.

Kimble, Joseph P. "Police Training Today and the Challenge for Tomorrow," *Police,* IX (September-October, 1964), 11-14.

As an instructor in Police Science at San Mateo College, the author feels that police training is at a "crossroads" where it must be decided whether local police departments are to continue their training independently or cooperate and experiment with new methods recommended by the author. He traces various internal and external influences on training and discusses changes he feels should be made in police training.

Kreml, Franklin M. *The Role of Colleges and Universities in Police Management: Address by . . . Before the International Association of Chiefs of Police, Miami Beach, Florida, October 6, 1965.* (1965), 14 pp.

In a speech before the International Association of Chiefs of Police, the author indicates barriers between the universities and the law enforcement agencies and suggests how they might be overcome, makes the distinction between education and training, discusses the reasons educated men are needed in police force, and enumerates ways in which the universities can help law enforcement agencies.

————. "What Types of Training or Educational Opportunities Are Essential to Provide Police Officers with the Knowledge and Skill Expected of Them?" *Traffic Digest and Review,* I (April, 1953), 6-10.

The author discusses his subject under four principal headings: general education, departmental in-service training, outside specialized training, and pre-service training.

Matt, A. Robert. "Officer Continuation Training," *Police,* V (September-October, 1960), 6-9.

This article focuses on the problem of officer continuation training and what should be taught including new laws, ideas and techniques, and manual skills.

————. "Police Firearms Training Programs," *Police,* IV (January-February, 1960), 72-74.

A discussion of the need to enlarge the scope of firearms training and extend hours devoted to it, to expand the available force of instructors, and the role of the police training officer.

Moseley, H. M. "Suggestions for In-Service Training in a Small Police Department," *Georgia Municipal Journal,* XII (March, 1962), 14-18.

The author deals with preliminary problems in establishing an off-duty, in-service training program for a small police department: budgeting, finding a place and time, locating qualified instructors, purchasing equipment and materials, obtaining training films, and selecting printed materials. A list of established schools where police officer training is available is provided.

Municipal Police Administration. Chicago: International City Managers' Association, 1961, 545 pp.

Chapter five of this text, used for an in-service training course on police administration offered by the Institue, discusses post induction and pre-employment training that is available to police officers. The range of topics includes general considerations, basic recruit training, advanced in-service training, specialized in-service training, and training methods.

Pomrenke, Norman E. "Minimum Standards for Police Training," *Popular Government,* XXXII (December, 1965), 20-21.

The first of a series on upgrading police training, this article focuses on what the minimum standards are and problems in minimum standards of training.

"Procedures and Training for One-Man Police Patrol Cars," *Management Information Service* (November, 1956), entire issue.

This report summarizes the steps needed for successful installation and operation of one-man police patrol cars, reviews the reorganization of patrol districts in several cities, and outlines the forms of training needed for patrolmen and dispatchers.

Purdy, E. Wilson. "The New American Way of Life Presents New Problems to Police Administrators: Urgent Need For More Police Training," *Pennsylvanian,* IV (March, 1965), 4-5.

The author suggests that municipalities should look upon the cost of police training as an investment—not an expense. The return on this investment is a more efficient, more effective police force which will produce a substantial reduction in the social and economic costs of crime, vice, juvenile delinquency, and traffic accidents.

"Rochester Plans College Course for Police Officers," *New York State Office for Local Government Newsletter,* V (May 30, 1966), 1, 3.

Covers a plan for training qualified high school graduates for appointment as police officers. It includes a two-year course at a community college, the State's basic training course, and part-time work in the Rochester Police Bureau.

Rogers, Howard L. " Are You Planning A Police Recruit Training Program?," *Police,* VI (January-February, 1962), 46-48.

The value of recording the procedures which go into developing a training program and the purposes of a procedural guide are discussed. Illustrations are given of what form such a guide might take.

————. "Determining Police Training Needs: In-Service," *Police,* VI (March-April, 1962), 55-61.

This article suggests the use of police job descriptions as a basis for determining training needs and includes several examples of job description resumes which might be adopted.

Siegel, Arthur I., Federman, Philip J., and Schultz, Douglas G. *Professional Police-Human Relations Training.* Springfield: Charles C. Thomas, Publishers, 1963, 161 pp.

A complete instructional package which can form the basis for a professional police-human relations training course.

It includes an instructor's or conference leader's manual, required case materials, and lecture outlines. The course is based on the case method of presentation.

Sommers, William A. "Practical Approach to Training in Peoria: Providing Adequate Training in the Smaller Department," *Police Chief,* XXIII (May, 1956), 14, 16, 18-20.

This article covers the ideas motivating the police training school, the point of view behind some of the subjects taught, the mechanics of setting up a school, interim training for recruits, and in-service and academic supervisory training.

"Special Training Helpful to Police in Sex Crimes," *FBI Law Enforcement Bulletin,* XXXI (July, 1962), 3-6.

This article covers such matters as obligations of the police, what a competent investigator must do, suspect possibilities, different methods of investigation, and what to search for in making investigations.

Stottler, Richard H. and others. "Police Personnel," *Police Yearbook.* Washington, D. C.: International Association of Chiefs of Police, 1961, 168-98.

Partial contents are: "A Beginning Without an End" by R. H. Stottler; "Report of Education and Training Committee" by R. R. J. Gallati; "Advanced In-Service Training" by D. A. McCandless; "Role of the FBI in Police Training" by J. S. Rogers; "A Weakness in Police Training" by R. L. Holcomb; and "Need for Accelerated Progress in Training" by B. C. Brannon.

Trimmer, Albert J. "Police Training: Present Status, Future Requirements," *Traffic Digest and Review,* (February, 1965), 10-13.

A discussion of police education and training—both pre-entry and post-entry—by the Director of the Training Division of the Northwestern University Traffic Institute. He also notes problems such as the failure to recognize need for and lack of facilities, and recommends a National Police Training Committee made up of top training officials from various states.

Whisenand, Paul M. "Equipping Men for Professional Development in the Police Service: The Federal Law Enforcement Assistance Act of 1965," *Journal of Criminal Law, Criminology, and Police Science,* LVII (June, 1966), 223-27.

The author recommends that those responsible for police training—government training officials and University deans and faculties—need a re-analysis of what a police officer does and of the value of in-service training and university training.

Woodson, C. W., Jr., and others. "Education and Training," *Police Yearbook.* Washington, D. C.: International Association of Chiefs of Police, 1953, 155-70.

The contents are: "The Practical Side of State Police Training Methods" by C. W. Woodson, Jr.; "Recruit Training" by I. B. Bruce; "Basic Police Practice and Procedure" by A. T. Smalley; and "Training of Auxiliary Police" by P. Purcell.

c. General References on Techniques of Training

Charman, H. R. "The Check-Off List as a Training Tool," *Public Personnel Review,* XIII (October, 1952), 179-85.

Emphasizes the importance of the check-off list in training programs, outlining the procedures for setting up a check-off list, operation of the system, method of training, and advantages and costs of a check-off list.

Diamond, Harry. "Factors in Planning and Evaluating In-Service Training Programs," *Journal of Criminal Law, Criminology, and Police Science,* LIII (December, 1962), 503-06.

Two basic considerations of an in-service training program are the determination of training needs and the subsequent evaluation of the training effort. The author describes the Crawford Slip technique for spotting needs, and the aspects which, if measured accurately, might give an indication of the value of a recently completed program.

Gammage, Allen Z. "Sound Recordings As Police Training Aids," *Police,* VI (July-August, 1962), 15-18; (May-June, 1963), 35-38.

Deals with the use of still projection in training and outlines the advantages and disadvantages in the use of projected materials, various types of projectors, and the method of teaching police subject matter with projected materials.

_____. "The Third Dimension in Police Training," *Police,* VI (March-April, 1962), 52-54.

This article discusses the use of three dimensional materials for initiating direct experience which cannot be provided in the classroom, describing models, mock-ups, specimens, and objects.

_____. "Training Police Through Motion Picture Films," *Police,* VII (September-October, 1962), 23-26.

The effective use of motion pictures in police training is dealt with including its special advantages and limitations, what films are available, and how and when to use them.

"A Giant Step: IACP Sight/Sound Training Filmstrips," *Police Chief,* XXXIII (January, 1966), 24-B - 24-F.

An announcement and description of a new tool for training police that can be used for roll call training, recruit training, and other purposes. It was designed by the International Association of Chiefs of Police and called the Sight/Sound Filmstrip Program.

Harrison, Leonard H. "Use of the Training Film," *Police,* VII (July-August, 1963), 75-77.

Training films are not fully effective unless instructors understand the function of this device as a part of a total program. The function of the training films, the elements of a lesson, and the method for transforming a film into an effective lesson are discussed.

Hollingsworth, Dan. "The Conference Method—A Stimulant for Police Management and Training," *Police,* II (September-October, 1957), 18-24.

Discusses the advantages of the conference method and duties and qualifications of the conference leader. It includes the author's definitions of "policies and procedure" of police departments which he considers the backbone of the conference method.

Muhlbach, George W. "Effective Lesson Planning and Presentation," *Police Chief,* XXXII (August, 1965), 48-49.

Elementary step-by-step advice is provided on how to prepare a lesson. The points made should prove equally useful for preparing a report of any type.

Peper, John P. "Audio Visual Training," *California Peace Officer,* XI (May-June, 1961), 33-38.

Discusses various types of visual and audio-visual aids and their use as part of a training program.

Police Training Films. Albany: Municipal Police Training Council, New York State Office for Local Government, 1967, 37 pp.

Divided into two parts, this publication lists films purchased by the Council and loaned by the New York State Office for Local Government Film Library and films which can be obtained from other agencies and their sources. The lists are preceded by information on how to use slides and films effectively.

Silverstone, David M. "Perception Training for Police," *Law and Order,* XIV (May, 1966), 44-45.

Techniques being used to improve perceptual skills of police officers including the basic instruments and kinds of material used with them. The author also gives suggestions for setting up a program.

Soule, Rolland L. "Role Playing—A New Police Training Tool," *Police,* IV (March-April, 1960), 19-22.

Role playing with its associated techniques offers an unlimited potential in the police training field, and in this article Mr. Soule develops the blueprint for its use by the police. The form for Instructor's Guide and Instructions for Observers is included.

_____. "The Use of Visual Aids in Training Identification Officers," *Journal of Criminal Law, Criminology, and Police Science,* LI (September-October, 1960), 363-72.

The author discusses nine different instructional aids—used by the author under controlled conditions—to teach students the techniques of classification and identification work.

"Training by TV," *Traffic Digest and Review,* X (January, 1962), 4-7.

Aspects of training police officers by television are discussed with reference to the New York City Police Department as the first to adopt television police training. Preliminary facts are given on benefits, cost, operation, and maintenance.

2. Cadet and Police Aide Programs

Bagley, Gerald L. "A Police Cadet Program for the City of Whittier," *Police,* X (September-October, 1965), 65-69; (November-December, 1965), 68-72.

A two-part article discussing the establishment of a cadet training program in Whittier, California. The first part concentrates on the preparation of the program and the recruitment of cadets, while the second part focuses on the program in action and an evaluation of effectiveness after one year of implementation. Included are a sample cadet evaluation test and cadet orientation schedule.

Block, Richard. "Milwaukee's Police Aide Program A Success: Apprenticeship Plan Offers High School Graduates Career Opportunities in the Police Service," *Public Personnel Review,* XIX (October, 1958), 276-78.

An evaluation of the country's first apprenticeship program within a police department, established in Milwaukee in

1952. The article deals with the importance of office skills, changing methods of recruitment, benefits, progress, and problems.

Carroll, Joseph T. "Recruiting and Training of Police Personnel," *FBI Law Enforcement Bulletin*, XXXIII (December, 1964), 3-8.

The Chief of Police of Lincoln, Nebraska discusses the cadet program which was instituted in 1960 to supplement the source of qualified applicants as patrolmen. Cadets were used as parking enforcers and for office routines while they were attending training sessions within the department and at the University of Nebraska. The author also discusses assignment of meter maids.

Fay, Lewis. "Revitalizing a Police Cadet Program," *Public Personnel Review*, XXIV (January, 1963), 60-62.

A case study of what was done in San Diego, California when it was realized that the city's relatively new personnel program was in trouble. The account indicates how the trouble could be located and the importance of views from other cities having cadet programs in revitalizing this program.

Flynn, Edward J., Holl, W. K., and Hartman, Earl P. *The Metropolitan Police Survey for the Board of Commissioners of the District of Columbia.* Washington, D. C.: Board of Commissioners Committee, District of Columbia, 1955, 53 pp.

Pertinent sections of this survey include a brief discussion of the Pasadena police cadet plan and material on the need for various types of training. Although intended for the use of the District of Columbia, much of the information is applicable generally.

Ocheltree, Keith. *Police Cadet Programs.* Chicago: Public Personnel Association, 1961, 8 pp.

Twelve police cadet programs are analyzed by means of a "question and answer" approach as well as by a comparative chart giving such facts as age limits, previous education required, length and content of programs, and other aspects.

O'Reiley, Patrick. "San Diego Establishes Police Cadet Program," *Police*, V (November-December, 1960), 6-9.

This article discusses the needs motivating the inception of the cadet program in San Diego, its purpose, the organization of the program, the program in action, and its development.

Police Aide Training Program. Milwaukee: Milwaukee Fire and Police Commission, February, 1952, 5 pp.

A description of a proposed four-year apprenticeship program. The elements of the selection process, qualifications, salary, and training program are outlined.

"Police Apprenticeship Program Pays Off in Milwaukee," *Police*, III (July-August, 1959), 59.

High school graduates may enter the Police Department as police aides until they meet the necessary age requirements. In the first year of service they attend vocational school in the morning for courses in typing, shorthand, English, and office practice. During the four year program, they perform clerical and other routine assignments.

"Police Cadet Program Inaugurated," *Arkansas Municipalities*, XXI (January, 1965), 14.

The Little Rock Police Department now hires high school

graduates of 19-21 to handle clerical and similar duties while they become familiar with law enforcement practices.

"Police Reserves and Cadets," *Proceedings of the 1959 Seminar, July 23-24, 1959, Police Administration.* Wichita: Center for Urban Studies, University of Wichita, 1959, 1-25.

A panel discussion covering the relative problems and advantages of using a cadet program or police reserves system to keep possible recruits interested in police work from the time they graduate from high school to age twenty-one. Some material on college training and the recruitment of college graduates is also covered.

Seares, Robert S. "The Police Cadet," *Annals*, CCXCI (January, 1954), 107-12.

The author discusses the concept of a police cadet plan emphasizing the needs such a plan would meet and the values of such a plan based on the English experience and the plans developed by the cities of Milwaukee and Kansas City.

Sorensen, Clyde A. "Police Cadet Program Provides Useful Recruitment Tool," *Minnesota Municipalities*, XLVII (1962), 286-88.

Discusses how to implement a cadet program, training of the cadet, and some problems of the program.

A Training Program in Human Relations for Cadet and In-Service Police Officers. Detroit: Police Academy, Detroit Police Department, April, 1952, 26 pp.

Outlines of the content and teaching method of four subjects in police training in human relations—information and ideas, attitudes and sensitivity, skills, and ways of thinking—broken down into six periods covering approximately eight hours.

3. Delinquency Control

Brennan, James J., and Olmstead, Donald W. *Police Work With Delinquents: Analysis of a Training Program.* East Lansing: Social Science Research Bureau, Michigan State University, 1965, 115 pp.

A description of a two-year project and its findings consisting of (1) an intensive three-week instructional program for police officers in the understanding, prevention, and control of juvenile delinquency and (2) a rigorous evaluation of the impact of the training program.

Carnes, Robert M., and Ryan, John W. *Police Training for Delinquency Prevention and Control.* Madison: Bureau of Government, Extension Division, University of Wisconsin, 1961, 45 pp.

A study of the effectiveness of juvenile delinquency prevention training programs, conducted during 1956-59 in Wisconsin, and their impact on local communities.

Cincinnati Demonstration for Inter-Agency Training, A Project of the Committee on Juvenile Delinquency Control . . . Final Report, May 1963 - May 1964. Cincinnati: Community Health and Welfare Council, 1964, 55 pp.

"The purpose of the demonstration has been to train police, juvenile court workers, school personnel, and public welfare staff to work more effectively with youth who may become delinquent." The workshop type of in-service training was used. The program began with a two day institute at a location away from the work location. This was followed by small group sessions of ninety minutes each twice weekly for six weeks and then once weekly for six weeks.

Delinquency Control and Prevention Training for Police Officers: Digest of Findings. Madison: Bureau of Government, Extension Division, University of Wisconsin, December, 1959, 6 pp.

A digest of principal findings and some general conclusions based on the data of a study initiated by the Bureau in June, 1959 which sought to evaluate the general effectiveness of the juvenile delinquency prevention training programs conducted during 1956-59, especially the Two-Week Delinquency Control Course for Law Enforcement Officers.

Gilman, Merritt Curtis. "Problems and Progress in Staff Training," *Crime and Delinquency,* XII (July, 1966), 254-60.

The progress made in training programs for police, probation, and parole officers, judges, and institutional personnel is discussed and the objectives of orientation and in-service training programs are analyzed in this article.

Greenblatt, Bernard. "Staff and Training for Juvenile Law Enforcement in Urban Police Departments," *Juvenile Delinquency: Facts and Facets.* Washington, D. C.: United States Government Printing Office, 1960.

This article is based on information obtained from a nationwide questionnaire survey conducted by the United States Children's Bureau. It covers staff, number and kinds of units, educational requirements for staff, and kinds of training.

Kennedy, John P., and others. *California Police Training Programs Relating to Juvenile Offenders: A Survey and A Perspective for Future Development.* Los Angeles: Youth Studies Center, University of Southern California, 1961, 33 pp.

This paper is divided into three sections: "a consideration of the complex and ambiguous nature of the police role in dealing with juveniles and consequent problems in developing training programs fitted to their responsibilities; the results of the Center's survey of California law enforcement training programs relating to juvenile offenders; and some reflections on training needs and next steps in meeting these needs, and a perspective for future development."

MacNamara, Donal E. J. "Value of Technical Police Training in the Prevention of Crime and Delinquency," *Journal of Criminal Law, Criminology, and Police Science,* XLII (July-August, 1951), 262-69.

The author feels that police training—except for a few admittedly outstanding programs—is generally much lower than what it should be and is generally thought to be. He discusses why this is so and what should be done about it.

"Police Training Practices Relating to Juvenile Delinquency," *Police Chief,* XXX (January, 1963), 29-30, 32.

Summarizes the replies of 242 police departments to a questionnaire sent to all communities with populations over 25,000.

Pursuit, Dan G. "Training for Juvenile Delinquency Control," *Police Chiefs News,* XVII (January, 1950), 19-24.

Provides general information on the Delinquency Control Institute at the University of Southern California—its purpose, organization, and curriculum.

Swab, Robert D., Jr. "County Level Institutes on Police Handling of Juveniles: Institutes Equip Police to Better Prevent and Control Juvenile Delinquency as Part of Planned Community Effort," *Pennsylvania Chiefs of Police Association Bulletin,* XXIII (Fall, 1962), 21, 31.

County institutes are sponsored by the local juvenile courts in cooperation with state offices and the Pennsylvania Chiefs of Police Association. The twenty-hour basic course is designed to benefit police administrators and personnel in providing increased services to children and their families and to prepare officers for advanced training in juvenile police work for departments large enough to have specialists or units.

————. "Police Juvenile Services Curricular Needs For In-Service Training," *Pennsylvania Chiefs of Police Association Bulletin,* XXVI (Summer, 1965), 12, 28-29.

Detailed outlines and suggestions to be considered in establishing a juvenile services program are presented. The outlines cover scope and objectives, determination of needs, resource materials, instructors, curriculum content, objectives, and evaluation and appraisal.

————. "Spring Training Programs," *Pennsylvania Chiefs of Police Association Bulletin,* XXVII (Summer, 1966), 8, 28.

The author describes the work of the State Bureau of Youth Services in cooperation with the Association in providing specialized training for police officers on a county, regional, and statewide basis with specific information on the two-week institutes held in Philadelphia and Pittsburgh.

Watson, Nelson A., and Walker, Robert N. *Training Police for Work with Juveniles.* Washington, D. C.: Research and Development Division, International Association of Chiefs of Police, December, 1965, 60 pp.

Methods of determining training needs, curriculum development, and suggested curricula are offered in this publication. A sample lesson plan format, list of films, and bibliography of suggested texts for use by instructors are included.

Wolke, Michael S. "Police Need Training in Problems of Youth," *Law and Order,* VII (October, 1959), 33-34.

The author advocates greater emphasis on training in "the science of human relations" for all law enforcement personnel with special emphasis on "crime prevention work."

4. Minority Group Relations

Brown, Albert N. "Philadelphia 'Operation Spanish'," *Police Chief,* XXIX (April, 1962), 20, 22, 24.

A report on Philadelphia's program to give its police officers a sound basic understanding of the language, customs, and history of the approximately 30,000 Puerto Ricans living in that city.

Cahill, Thomas J. "Seminar: Police Training for Inter-Racial Problems," *Police Chief,* XXX (December, 1963), 34-37.

The Chief of Police of San Francisco, California discusses the need for new law enforcement techniques, methods, and personnel qualifications necessary to cope with the civil rights and racial problems. He describes some of his city's training programs designed to meet the need.

Epstein, Charlotte. *Intergroup Relations for Police Officers.* Baltimore: Williams & Wilkins Company, 1962, 194 pp.

This book covers intergroup relations and police work; how and what people learn; how people learn prejudice; scientific approach to intergroup relations; significance of racial, religious, and nationality differences; some facts about racial, religious, and nationality differences and about intergroup relations; some effects of prejudice and discrimination; prejudice, discrimination, and human nature; and the American tradition of equality.

A Guide to Understanding Race and Human Relations . . . for Police Instructional Purposes. Milwaukee: Mayor's Commission on Human Rights, 1952, 31 pp.

The contents cover understanding race and human relations, what prejudice is, the facts about race, civil rights and civil liberties laws, the role of the police officer in understanding and dealing with human relation problems, mob and crowd behavior, rumors, and a summation.

Lawler, Irvin D. *A Training Program in Human Relations for Cadet and In-Service Police Officers.* Detroit: Police Academy, Detroit Police Department, April 1, 1952, 26 pp.

This outline, prepared for use of the Detroit Police Academy, presents step-by-step the content and methods of instruction to be employed in an eight-hour course on minority groups and police relations with such groups.

McManus, George P. "Human Relations Training for Police," *Journal of Criminal Law, Criminology, and Police Science,* XLVI (May-June, 1955), 105-11.

The author, who is the member of the New York City Police Academy preparing and presenting the Department's program on human relations training, discusses the significance of the training and describes the program. Areas covered by the program are background culture, national origin, and religion of the city's people; shortcomings and personality deficiencies of the officer himself; his responsibility to the community; his personal prejudices; understanding facts about crowd formation and mob psychology; and consideration of civil rights laws and guarantees.

"Race and Law Enforcement: A Guide to Modern Police Practices," *New South* (February, 1952), entire issue.

An analysis presenting some of the problems of race and law enforcement in a positive and practical light, and providing a guide for civic-minded people.

A Study of Police Training Programs in Minority Relations. Los Angeles: Southern California Regional Office, Anti-Defamation League of B'nai B'rith, August, 1950, 28 p.

This study summarizes activities in twenty-two cities from 1943 to 1950. The essentials of a good program are listed and a recommended program for Los Angeles is presented. Very brief descriptions of the programs of individual cities and a four-page bibliography of printed and audio-visual materials are appended.

5. Riot Control

Administrative Seminar. Lexington, Kentucky: Lexington Police Department, 1966, 107 pp.

The twenty-nine lessons reproduced here discuss social be-

havior in mobs, civil disorders, riots, and strikes and include case histories of racial disorders, and lengthy instructions to the Lexington Police Department for handling civil disturbances.

Gray, Richard D. "Riot Control Demonstration," *Pennsylvania Chiefs of Police Association Bulletin,* XXV (Fall, 1964), 21, 32.

Describes a one-day institute on "Crowd Control and Riot Formation," held at the Pennsylvania State Police Academy in Hershey, Pennsylvania for police chiefs and supervising personnel from a six-county area.

Havlick, J. Robert. "Training and Equipping Police Crowd and Riot Control Officers and Units," *Management Information Service* (May, 1966), entire issue.

This article covers guidelines and suggestions including length and frequency of programs, desirable characteristics of officers engaged in crowd and riot control, basic elements of a curriculum on this subject, physical aspects of such training, officer self-defense, use of riot equipment, squad formation training, and equipping the officer and the unit.

Kline, James S. "Crowd and Riot Control Requires Special Training," *FBI Law Enforcement Bulletin,* XXXIII (October, 1964), 8-12.

The Coordinator of Police Training at the Governmental Research Center at the University of Kansas describes how a riot at Garnett, Kansas brought about constructive action in the planning of a two-day training program for police in crowd and riot control techniques.

Leonard, Glenford G. "Our Tactical Police Unit," *Police Chief,* XXIX (April, 1962), 34-37.

A discussion of the steps taken to organize and train a special police unit in the special techniques of riot control.

6. Traffic Control

Davin, Frank. "The World Is Their Beat: 'West Point of Traffic Policing' Trains Men for Duty at Home and Around the Globe," *Traffic Safety,* LIX (October, 1961), 10-13.

This article describes the impact of training taken at the Traffic Institute of Northwestern University.

Developing a Better Traffic Supervision Program. Evanston: Traffic Institute, Northwestern University, no date, 12 pp.

A brochure outlining the direct technical assistance the Institute can give government agencies to help them improve the effectiveness of motor vehicle supervision.

Fundamentals of Traffic Engineering: Syllabus. Berkeley: Institute of Transportation and Traffic Engineering, University of California, 1963.

A detailed outline for University courses in traffic engineering.

Gallien, Shelby. "Effective Police Traffic Training," *Traffic Quarterly,* VII (October, 1953), 531-39.

This article discusses the magnitude of the traffic control problem and the need for training. It presents a historical background in police training including origins of today's university programs and suggests whose responsibility it is to provide training and lists the various kinds of training.

"Highway Patrol Training—1959," *Popular Government,* LIX (November, 1959), 14-15.

> The North Carolina State Highway Patrol Schools include refresher in-service training for commissioned and non-commissioned officers and patrolmen, ranging from thirty to forty hours each, and the twelve-week basic training school in traffic law enforcement.

Hoover, John Edgar. "Police Training for Traffic Control," *Traffic Quarterly,* I (October, 1947), 301-11.

> This article covers what the author believes should be included in the training of traffic officers and why.

Jacobs, David L. G. "The Challenge of Training for Non-Routine Tasks: How to Train the New Employee Who Must Exercise Considerable Judgment in Varied Situations Far Removed From Close Supervision," *Public Personnel Review,* XIX (July, 1958), 177-82.

> Using the work done at the Northwestern University Traffic Institute as an example of the method for training the "versatile" employee, this article focuses on establishing criteria for complex tasks, planning a variety of training situations, and manuals.

Latchaw, James A. "Assistance for State Police Training," *Law and Order,* XIV (July, 1966), 42-43.

> Describes why, how, and where the Insurance Institute for Highway Safety provides financial assistance in training for selected individual police agencies.

Noffsinger, Forest R. "Traffic Institute's Training Option Teaches Relationship To Management," *Police,* IX (May-June, 1965), 93-95.

> Based on the experience of Northwestern University's Traffic Institute's Training in Methods and Programs for Police, this article deals with determining training need, types of training programs, tailoring a course to determine need, techniques of teaching, and evaluation.

Promotional and Procedural Guide for Traffic Short Courses and Conferences. Chicago: Traffic Education and Training Committee, National Safety Council, 1961, 43 pp.

> Treats in chronological order the steps which normally should be taken in preparing for and conducting short course training. The Appendix includes samples of several forms.

"The Right Man with the Right Training," *Traffic Digest and Review,* X (May, 1962), 11-12.

> A report on how training paid off in lives saved and an overall reduction in traffic accidents. A Springfield, Missouri police officer, following techniques learned at the Traffic Institute of Northwestern University, plotted out where and when most accidents occurred. By concentrating police efforts on these times and places, accidents dropped sharply.

Schrotel, Stanley R. "Training Fosters Ideals of Professionalism," *Traffic Digest and Review,* XII (August, 1964), 16-17.

> The author feels law enforcement training should be made a professional educative process.

Thriscutt, Herbert Sydney. "The Training of Traffic Engineers," *Traffic Quarterly,* XVII (July, 1962), 410-20.

> This article covers lecturer's background, planning of courses, kinds of students, building a reference library, equipment needed, and the syllabus.

A Training Manual on the Application of the Uniform Enforcement Policy (A Complete Traffic Law Enforcement System for Accident Prevention): Basic Principles of Traffic Law Enforcement Upon Which the Uniform Enforcement Policy Is Based. Evanston, Ill.: International Association of Chiefs of Police, 1947, 33 pp.

> A manual covering the background of the development of the uniform enforcement policy, its past and future use, basic traffic law principles, and instructions for conducting a six-day training school for police who will use the system.

Trimmer, Albert J. "Police Training: Present Status, Future Requirements," *Traffic Digest and Review,* XIII (February, 1965), 10-13.

> A discussion of police education and training—both pre-entry and post-entry—by the Director of the Training Division of the Northwestern University Traffic Institute. He also notes problems such as the failure to recognize need and lack of facilities, and recommends a National Police Training Committee made up of top training officials from various states.

H. Public Relations

Anderson, Desmond L. (ed.) *Municipal Public Relations.* Chicago: International City Managers' Association, 1966, 273 pp.

> Provides students and local government administrators with a better understanding of public relations within the context of the governmental process and acquaints them with some of the more sophisticated aspects of public relations as well as the practices and techniques of public information.

Costello, Michael. "Municipal 'Charm School': Milwaukee Teaches Its Public Servants How to Get Along With Their Bosses, the Taxpayers, During the Day's Work," *National Municipal Review,* XLIII (May, 1954), 230-34.

> The author discusses the development and effectiveness of special classes conducted by the City of Milwaukee to teach its employees how to deal pleasantly and efficiently with the public and with one another. Specific examples from class discussions as well as an evaluation of the program are presented.

"Film Sparks PR Training, "*American City,* LXXX (August, 1965), 140, 142-43.

> A film entitled "I Just Work Here" is used by Glendale, California as the central training tool in its public relations course. Five weekly sessions are held, usually during work hours. The film first presents negative handling of situations and then a proper approach.

Groos, Arthur B. "Training and Public Relations in Government," *Personnel Administration,* XIII (November, 1950), 8-11.

> An argument for the need to improve public relations between the public and government services. Suggested are

types of public relations instruction, specific public relations activities for training specialists, and opportunities for consultative technical services having public relations value.

Hayworth, Thadene. "Public Relations Training for Public Employees," *Public Personnel Review,* X (January, 1949), 17-22.

The author describes the development of a public relations training program organized by the Los Angeles Region of the California Association of Drivers' License Examiners and employees of the California Department of Motor Vehicles. In addition, a broader statement of the policies and procedures which should be considered in developing a public relations training program in any jurisdiction is set forth.

Hunger, John M., and Schten, Edward V. "Training the Public Administrator in Public Relations," *Training Directors Journal,* XVIII (January, 1964), 37-40.

The program of a one-day institute on public relations for public officials in Wisconsin organized and presented by the Bureau of Government of the University of Wisconsin is covered, together with the results of the questionnaire sent to enrollees "to ascertain their reactions to the Insitute and to identify officials' perceptions of needs for future educational efforts concerning public relations."

Huntley, Robert J. *A Public Relations Training Course for Municipal Employees.* Chicago: Government Public Relations Association, February, 1957, 27 pp.

Complete information on the course, from how it was developed through schedules, outlines, and lecture material, to bibliography.

"Milwaukee Has a 'Charm School'—PR Course for City Employees," *American City,* LXVIII (August, 1953), 124.

A public relations card was issued to each employee upon completion of the course, conducted on working time. The course is planned by the city officials and the Milwaukee Vocational School. Informal instructional materials are used in the eight one-hour conferences.

Municipal Public Relations: Short Course. Philadelphia: Institute of Local and State Government, University of Pennsylvania, 1947.

A series of four-page leaflets issued for each subject covered in the one-day course. The subjects include nature of public relations, employee-citizen contacts, governmental procedures, physical appearance, training employees in public relations, publicity and press relations, municipal reports, and citizen participation.

"Training City Employees in Public Relations," *Management Information Service* (June, 1955), entire issue.

Ways are suggested as to how a city can further its public relations program by in-service training of its employees. It is based, in part, on extensive programs developed and carried out in Jackson, Michigan; Norfolk, Virginia; and Beverly Hills, California.

White, Larry C. "Employees Public Relations Program Puts City's 'Best Foot Forward,'" *Western City,* XXX (January, 1954), 27, 49.

An outline of the purposes, procedures, course content, and advantages of the public relations program developed in Glendale, California.

I. Public Works

American Public Works Association Yearbook. Chicago: American Public Works Association, 1964, 580 pp.
A section of this publication contains addresses by five panel speakers at the 1963 Congress of the Association on: "The Need for In-Service Training Increasing;" "The Technical Nature of Public Works Positions," "Public Administration Educational Programs for the Public Works Official," and "Administrative and Supervisory Aspects of Public Works Positions."

Chicago Civil Service Commission, and the Department of Streets and Sanitation. *Ward Superintendents Conference Manual.* Chicago: Civil Service Commission, 1965, 201 pp.

This describes the content and format of the seven units of the series: Introduction, City Organization, Department of Streets and Sanitation, Bureau of Equipment Service, Bureau of Sanitation, Ward and Division Superintendents, and Civil Service Commission.

"Chicago's In-Service Training Program," *Building Standards Monthly* (August, 1955), 7-9.

Reviews the history and activities of the Advisory Committee on In-Service Training of Chicago's Building Department, evaluates the in-service training program, and presents recommendations for future training activities.

"Commissioners Enthusiastic About Georgia County Workshop," *Better Roads,* LII (February, 1962), 15-17.

A description of the content of two sessions—Organization of the State Highway Department, and Planning, Constructing, and Maintaining County Roads—of the experimental workshop established to provide general information for county commissioners relating to their duties in local government.

The Construction and Financing of Town Buildings. Albany: The Association of Towns of the State of New York, 1959, 61 pp.

Prepared by the staff of the Association as part of its program of education and in-service training of town officers, this manual discusses procedures, law, and forms.

Cron, Robert E., Jr. "In-Service Training for Public-Works Inspectors," *Better Roads,* LIII (July, 1963), 12-14.

This article describes a thirty-hour course presented on Friday nights and Saturday mornings for five weekends. The course was taught by professional men in the field and planned and developed by a committee of the Northern California Chapter of the American Public Works Association. Subject matter, instructors, and sessions for the Berkeley campus course are listed.

————. "Street Maintenance—Supervision, Training and Academic Requirements," *American Public Works Association Reporter* (December, 1963), 4-7.

Management supervision principles are discussed as they can be applied to street maintenance. The author indicates the variety of academic requirements among American cities and suggests guidelines for in-service training programs.

"Detroit Sends Construction Inspectors to School," *Street Engineering* (October, 1959), 50-52.

A series of twenty-five man inspector classes were planned thoroughly as to choice of subject matter, preparation by instructors, and advance briefing. A careful evaluation was to follow.

Duba, John G. "American Public Works Association's Executive Development Program," *American Public Works Association Yearbook*, 1966, 307-12.

The Chairman of the Association's Education Foundation describes its four-point program designed to meet short and long term needs. He includes information on the Master of Public Works degree, Graduate Center for Public Works at the University of Pittsburgh, the APWA Public Works Engineer Management Trainee Program in cooperation with communities, public works management seminars, and in-service training programs.

Experiment in Extension Programs for County Highway Engineers. Washington, D. C.: Highway Research Board, National Research Council, 1953, 16 pp.

Describes the annual, four-day "Minnesota County Highway Engineers' Institute" held by the Minnesota County Highway Engineers' Association in conjunction with the University of Minnesota's Extension Division to acquaint highway engineers with the latest developments in highway administration.

Fairlie, P. D. "Recruitment and Training of Public Cleansing Supervisors," *Public Cleansing and Salvage,* (February, 1955), 91-102.

Glasgow's Director of Cleansing reports on methods used to recruit and train supervisors. Article also includes the syllabus for the Glasgow course of study and two of the examinations given.

Gallagher, Richard. "In-Service Training vs. the Manpower Shortage Problem," *Street Engineering* (June 1956), 26-27.

The author, who is Director of Public Works of San Diego, suggests in-service training as one of seven methods for coping with the manpower shortage. He believes basic courses in human relations and work simplication should be given first to present and potential supervisors.

Graham, Jack J. "Comments," *American Public Works Association Yearbook,* 1966, 318-21.

A description of the summer schedule for an engineer trainee in Fort Worth, Texas, excerpts from his report, and the author's comparison of this experience with the original concept of the Engineer/Management Trainee Program of the American Public Works Association.

Handbook of Construction Inspection, Reference Material and Notes for the In-Service Training Program. Honolulu: Honolulu Department of Civil Service, 1954.

This handbook lists the thirteen subjects taught in the course.

Hoag, James F. "Employees Learn How to Read Highway Plans in a Self-Taught Course," *Better Roads,* LV (May, 1965), 12-15.

A report on Iowa's first experience with programmed instruction methods for teaching inspectors and their engineering supervisors how to read highway plans.

Klein, Robert N. "Responsibility of Public Works Officer for Training in His Department," *Proceedings of the Public Works Officers' Institute, Monterey, California, April 16-17, 1959.* Berkeley: League of California Cities, 1959, 4 pp.

This speech was concerned primarily with on-the-job supervision as a training technique and emphasized the idea that this is a working lifetime process. The Proceedings as a whole cover a two-day Institute aimed at giving public works personnel a broader management view.

Municipal Public Works Administration, 5th ed. Chicago: International City Managers' Association, 1957, 449 pp.

Procedures and techniques are described which can be applied in the management of municipal public works treating the administrative aspects of the department and its correlation with other departments and with local government as a whole.

The Office of Town Highway Superintendent, Responsibilities and Administrative Procedures. Albany: The Association of Towns of the State of New York, 1964.

A manual which is used as the basic text for the home study course for town highway superintendents.

Principal Papers Presented at . . . Annual Public Works Training School. Albany: Conference of Mayors and Other Municipal Officials of the State of New York, Annual.

Co-sponsored by Cornell University, this publication contains papers on topics such as "On the Job Training," "Anti-Skid Pavements," and "Current Trends in Street and Highway Lighting Practices."

The Purchase and Financing of Town Highway Machinery. Albany: The Association of Towns of the State of New York, 1958, 77 pp.

An in-service training manual which discusses the law and procedures for purchasing and financing town highway machinery.

Reilly, Donald F. "Upgrading Employee Skills in Massachusetts," *Public Personnel Review,* XXVIII (July, 1967), 182-83.

This article describes Massachusetts' two-step solution to its shortage of trained engineers, namely, through training of technicians, and a five-year Associate in Engineering Degree course. Legislation permitted city and town employees to participate.

Sanderson, B. M. "In-Service Training Program Improves Skills and Raises Morale of Highway Employees," *Better Roads,* LV (June, 1965), 14-16.

The personnel chief of the New Mexico Highway Department describes its training program in general and a few parts in detail and points out the value of the program.

Sarvis, Robert G. "Employee Training Pays in Cincinnati," *Public Works Engineers' Newsletter,* XX (January, 1954), 1, 8-9.

A general discussion of in-service training for municipal employees, illustrated by specific examples from the programs of the Cincinnati Highway Maintenance Division for such employees as foremen and truck drivers.

School for Highway Superintendents. Albany: Town and County Officers Training School of the State of New York, 1967, 9 pp.

This pamphlet contains the program of the School for Highway Superintendents held at Cornell University, July 10-12, 1967 and sponsored by the Town and County Officers Training School of the State of New York.

Stone, Donald C. "Educational Underpinning for the Public Works Profession," *American Public Works Association Yearbook,* 1966, 313-17.

The author cites conditions required for launching professional education, describes eleven favorable factors for public works education, and outlines aspects of the American Public Works Association Pittsburgh program—its Graduate Center for Public Works, the degree programs, the specially designed curriculum, the short term, in-service training, research components, funding, and fellowships.

J. Parks and Recreation

Barrows, Walter J. *Practical Steps in Park and Recreation In-Service Training.* Berkeley: Recreation and Park Officials' Department, October 21, 1953, 7 pp.

This talk lists training goals and conditions essential to an effective in-service training program. Attached are short bibliographies, including training manuals and films, and lists of training institutes, related organizations, and agencies.

Charters, Werrett Wallace, and Fry, Vaughan W. *The Ohio Study of Recreation Leadership Training.* Columbus, Ohio: Bureau of Educational Research, Ohio State University, 1942, 173 pp.

Describes in detail the duties of recreation leaders, lists activities used in recreation programs, summarizes the recreation leader's personal qualities which are considered essential, and constructs a college course based on the information collected.

DaCosta, Robert C. "Training Program Aids Public Officials," *Tennessee Government,* IX (September-October, 1950), 1, 3.

A report on a series of regional conferences held in Tennessee for different local government groups—municipal finance officers, recreation board members, and Tennessee Rural Electric Cooperative Trustees.

Eppley, Garrett G. "In-Service Training," *Recreation,* XLVI (March, 1953), 616-17.

Together with recommendations of a sub-committee on in-service training of the National Recreation Association, the author lists fifteen objectives of an in-service training program and discusses training resources offered by institutes and colleges.

"In-Service Training," *Municipal Recreation Administration.* Chicago: International City Managers' Association, 1960, 304-10.

Objectives to be attained by in-service training are listed

Stoner, John E. "Training Programs in Connecticut, Michigan, and Ohio—A Comparison," *American Highways,* XXX (October, 1951), 9, 20-21.

This is a comparative study of highway training programs, made under a grant for this study from Indiana University.

Training and Development of Public Works Employees. Chicago: American Public Works Association, 1957, 51 pp.

A general survey of the need for trained personnel in public works and the necessity for up-grading the skills of available personnel in light of the continuing shortage of skilled personnel.

Trezise, Fred W. "Training Engineering Technicians," *Better Roads,* XLVIII (May, 1958), 21-22, 42, 44.

The background, development, administration, and content of the training course are covered.

Winfrey, Robley. "Education and Training for Highway Engineering Employees," *Traffic Quarterly,* XI (October, 1957), 557-72.

The author discusses the need for training and suggests that basic areas of a well-organized program would include (1) a specific plan for the technician, (2) an initial training schedule for college graduates, and (3) a program of refresher courses and review of the latest developments for technicians and college graduates. Appendices give details of (1) and (2). A bibliography is included.

in this chapter with brief discussions of training institutes, staff meetings, and other training methods. A detailed schedule for a pre-season institute for summer playground workers is included.

Intergroup Relations for Recreation Workers: Outline of an In-Service Training Institute. Washington, D. C.: American Friends Service Committee, March, 1954, 22 pp.

A detailed outline of an institute held for the District of Columbia Recreation Department. Included are a list of suggested experts and consultants, a list of national and local organizations, and an eleven-page bibliography on prejudice and minority groups in the United States.

Mid-Continent Regional Park and Recreation Conference (Second and Third) In-Service Training Institute (s), March 9-11, 1953 and March 6-9, 1955. Minneapolis: Center for Continuation Study, University of Minnesota, 1953-55.

Addresses, and summaries of discussions on physical, social, and administrative aspects of parks and recreation.

Municipal Recreation Administration, 4th ed. Chicago: International City Managers' Association, 1960, 409 pp.

Basic principles of recreation administration are illustrated in the programs of cities and other local governments. The authors also provide practical suggestions for putting these principles into effect.

Park Education Program: A Program to Improve Park and Recreation Administration. Chicago: American Institute of Park Executives, 1953, 11 pp.

Contains details of the program including its past preparation, purpose, and scope; agreement with its joint sponsor, Michigan State College; proposed projects; and financing.

Principal Papers Presented at Outdoor Recreation Seminar. Albany: Conference of Mayors and Other Municipal Officials of the State of New York, June, 1967.

Sponsored by the Conference of Mayors and Other Municipal Officials of the State of New York in cooperation with the New York State Department of Conservation and the New York State Department of Audit and Control, this publication contains papers on "The Federal Land and Water Conservation Fund Act," "Aid for the Development of Municipal Recreation Facilities and Historic Sites," "Marines Facilities Program Under the 200 Million Dollar Bond Issue," and "The Outdoor Recreation Program."

Proceedings of the Annual Park Short Course. . . Gainesville: General Extension Division, University of Florida, Annual.

Sponsored since 1950 by the Florida Association of Park Personnel, the course prepares park professionals for active roles in the field of development, maintenance, and operation of recreation-use lands. The suggestion is made that the Proceedings be used as an in-service training course for park employees. In 1965, the title of the organization was changed to The Florida Institute of Park Personnel, Inc.

Recreation in California: Institutes for Recreation Leaders. Sacramento: California Recreation Commission, 1948, 40 pp.

Describes the organization and operation of leadership training institutes including basic considerations, institute committees, schedules, and special problems.

Romilly, Edgar P. "A Good Administrator Knows the Importance of In-Service Training," *Park Maintenance,* XIV (September, 1961), 8-13.

This article defines in-service training, indicates when and where it should be used, cites advantages to the employee and the park, lists basic knowledge needed by the employee, and suggests subject content of training sessions. It also includes, in outline form, "A Simple Procedure for the Beginning of In-Service Training in a Small Park District."

_____. "In-Service Training for Park Employees," *Recreation,* XLIII (October, 1950), 251-54.

The author discusses the advantage of an in-service training program, describes nine categories of information to be covered, makes suggestions for organizing a program and the training methods to use, and indicates which subjects should be taught to supervisors.

Smith, Julian W. "Training Institutes for Voluntary Leaders in Camping and Outdoor Education," *Parks and Recreation,* XXXVII (June, 1954), 2, 20-21.

A discussion of various approaches for providing volunteer camp leaders with training in outdoor recreation work.

K. Water and Sewage

Cassler, Donald E. "Training Sewage Treatment Plant Operators," *Pennsylvanian: The Magazine of Local Governments,* IV (August, 1965), 14-15.

A discussion of the need for training of personnel of new plants, especially in biological and chemical processes. It surveys the kinds of training courses available in the state and what organizations provide them.

Faust, Raymond J. "In-Service Training and Certification," *Journal of the American Water Works Association,* XLIX (October, 1957), 1288-293.

After emphasizing the need for more highly-trained personnel to operate automatic equipment, the author gives a brief history of water utilities' in-service training, describes the present kinds available, and ties in the recommendations of the Committee on Education of the American Water Works Association. He also presents the recommendations from the Committee's report on Certification.

Hands, Glenn. "Water and Sewerage Training School," *American City,* LXXV (September, 1960), 97-99.

The technical school at Neosho, Missouri—sponsored by the Missouri Water and Sewerage Conference and supported by contributions from industry, consulting engineers, and the utilities—offered in 1960 a one-week technical course designed to train operators for specific licenses issued by the Conference Board of Examiners. The training equipment was supplied by manufacturers, municipalities, and utilities.

Ingram, William T. "Trained Operators—A Municipal Responsibility," *Journal of the American Water Works Association,* XLIV (July, 1952), 648-54.

Describes various training programs provided in New York State by the State Health Department and the Municipal Training Institute for water works operators.

"On-the-Job Training in Water Utilities: A Joint Discussion Presented on May 22, 1963, at the Annual Conference, Kansas City, Missouri," *Journal of the American Water Works Association,* LVI (April, 1964), 378-86.

The purpose of the discussion was to encourage and enable utility managers to initiate new programs or rejuvenate existing ones. A scheduled training program of Johnson City, New York was discussed, with emphasis on how it has helped both worker and teacher. Major objectives of employee training were outlined and the value and types of on-the-job training were discussed.

"An Outline for An On-The-Job Training Program for Water Department Personnel," *Public Works,* IV (July, 1947), 38-40, 42, 44, 46, 49-50, 52.

These summaries of outlines for the preparation of lessons or lectures for the program are organized into nine principal divisions and forty-three individual lectures with text references and instruction aids.

Proceedings of the Louisiana Conference on Water Supply and Sewerage: Annual Short Course for Superintendents and Operators of Water and Sewerage Systems . . . Baton Rouge: Louisiana State University and Agricultural and Mechanical College, Engineering Experiment Station, Annual.

Contains papers and minutes of the annual Short Courses. The first two or two and one-half days are general meetings and separate instructional sessions, and the third day is devoted to certification examinations for the various grades of operators according to the voluntary certification plan of the Conference.

Proceedings . . . Sewage Works Operators Short Course . . . Madison: Engineering Experiment Station, University of Wisconsin, Annual.

Contains a selection of the papers presented in the proceedings.

Proceedings . . . Water Works Operators Short Course . . . Madison: Engineering Experiment Station, University of Wisconsin, Annual.

Contains selected papers presented at the school.

Richmond, Maurice S., and Pierce, Donald M. "Operator Training and Certification in Michigan," *Journal of the Water Pollution Control Federation,* XXXVII (December, 1963), 1529-534.

The history of certification in Michigan, its present status, and its related educational programs are analyzed by two members of the Michigan State Department of Health.

Schwer, Arthur E., Jr. "Training Procedures for Plant Operators," *Journal of the Water Pollution Control Federation,* XXXVI (February, 1962), 184-88.

A detailed description of the training given sewage plant operators in Cincinnati before they are placed on the job.

L. Welfare

1. Surveys, Descriptions, and Analyses of Local Training Needs, Resources, and Programs

Black, John S. "The Value of In-Service Training As Education," *Child Welfare,* XXXVII (February, 1958), 19-24.

The Cuyahoga County Welfare Department in-service training program is described. "By using imaginatively the skills we have developed over the years, we can develop training programs which will not substitute for professional education, but will, where supervision is good, insure an acceptable quality of service."

Bradshaw, Estelle B. "Training For Full Utilization of Staff," *Employment Security Review,* XIX (February, 1952), 27-28.

The Virginia program for training local office employees is described. Local training is combined with a two-week group course in basic interviewing techniques, with a follow-up visit from a technician to give technical assistance as necessary.

Burford, Elizabeth. "A Formalized Homemaker Training Program," *Child Welfare,* XLI (September, 1962), 313-17.

The Child and Family Services Agency, a private Chicago agency, provides orientation training by a standard course of instruction presented by the supervisor and by observation of experienced homemakers. In-service training of experienced workers is given thorough individual supervision, group training courses, and individual instruction for special assignments. The group training courses for homemakers from four Chicago agencies are presented by the University of Illinois School of Social Work.

Burmeister, Eva. "Training For Houseparents," *Child Welfare,* XXXVI (January, 1957), 27-32.

A brief discussion of the need for training programs and of training programs within the institutions, followed by a more

Sopp, George C. "Improvement of Work Performance Through a Utility Training Program," *Journal of the American Water Works Association,* LVI (September, 1964), 1097-1104.

Training programs such as apprenticeship, customer service, orientation, and management development of the Los Angeles Department of Water and Power are described.

"Status of Training Courses and Certification in the United States," *Journal of the American Water Works Association,* XLV (September, 1953), 971-87.

This article covers the philosophy of a training program, short courses, special and extension courses, certification, recommendations and conclusions, various tables, and an appendix tabulating the requirements for certification in twenty-three states.

Van Heuvelen, W., and Lalonde, Lawrence E. "Training Water Works Personnel: Joint Discussion," *Journal of the American Water Works Association,* XLVIII (October, 1956), 1295-1300.

Describes objectives and techniques, and in-service programs in the training of water-works personnel.

extended description of semester-long courses presented by Washington and Saint Louis Universities in Saint Louis.

Chapel Hill Workshops, 1962: Part 1: Reports of the Sixteenth Annual Workshops for Houseparents and Others Caring for Children in Institutions . . . July 16-20, 1962. Chapel Hill: School of Social Work, University of North Carolina, 1962, 64 pp.

Includes addresses made at the general sessions and reports of the house-parents on the six writing committees in summing up the deliberations of their groups.

Chapel Hill Workshops, 1962: Part 2: Reports of the Eighteenth Annual Workshops for Executives and Other Administrative Personnel in Children's Institutions . . . July 23-27, 1962. Chapel Hill: School of Social Work, University of North Carolina, 1962, 56 pp.

Includes reports on the five workshops and papers prepared by panelists and general session speakers.

Clendenen, Richard J., and Cosby, Elizabeth M. "Staff Development in Kentucky . . . A Training Center for Child Welfare Staff," *Children* (March-April, 1964), 65-69.

A description of the planning and preparation for the residential training center of the Kentucky Department of Child Welfare, its physical plant, content and teaching methods used in courses, and an evaluation of the center.

"Conferences to Develop Staff Skills Held by Welfare Board Supervisors," *Welfare Reporter* (February, 1949), 9-10.

These round table conferences for case work supervisors in the administration of old age assistance were held in New Jersey. The first four sessions analyzed the worker's job. Consideration of the job of a supervisor is to follow.

Costin, Lela B. "Supervision and Consultation in the Licensing of Family Homes: The Use of Nonprofessional Personnel," *Child Welfare,* XLVI (January, 1967), 10-15.

The author reports on the performance of non-professional personnel in giving supervision and consultation to licensed foster mothers and day care operators, and draws conclusions regarding the effective training of such personnel.

————. "Training Nonprofessionals for a Child Welfare Service," *Children* (March-April, 1966), 63-68.

Article focuses on the results of a three-year cooperative training program undertaken by the University of Illinois School of Social Work and ten state public child welfare agencies to deal with the latter's role in licensing family homes for child care.

Cottage Parent Institute: Jacksonville, Illinois, September 1-2, 1960. Springfield: Illinois Department of Public Welfare, 1960, 14 pp.

Includes a speech on "Social Maturity" followed by Discussion Group A on social maturity in children to age thirteen, and Discussion Group B on social maturity in adolescents.

The Current Status of Staff Development in Public Assistance Agencies. Chicago: Illinois Public Aid Commission, 1954, 14 pp.

Report covers results of and statistics from a questionnaire sent to forty-eight states, four territories, and the District of Columbia asking questions about staff training, plus some of the conclusions drawn from the study.

Dubin, Julia. "Group Process in Supervisory Development," *Public Welfare,* XI (January, 1953), 16-19.

The author deals with the success of a supervisory seminar conducted by the Chicago Department of Welfare focusing on its purpose, method of organization, outline of meetings, and critique of the program.

Humphrey, Jackson C. "A Novel Scholarship Program for a Smaller City," *Family Service Highlights* (February, 1961), 47-49.

Describes St. Joseph, Missouri's plans for attracting recruits to the field of social work by offering scholarships, the publicity used, and the results achieved.

In-Service Training Course Lectures by the Executive Staff: Part 1, Seven Lectures, Winter-Spring Session 1939. New York: New York City Department of Welfare, 1939, 87 pp.

The course, designed by the executive staff to inform new employees of the responsibilities and operations of the Department, covers the history of welfare legislation and organization and operation of the various divisions.

Jensen, D. A., and Duren, Mary E. "Social Work Education for Public Welfare Employees: The Fresno Plan," *Public Welfare,* XIII (January, 1955), 18-21, 34.

A description of an experiment in social work education carried out jointly by the School of Social Welfare of the University of California and the Fresno County Department of Welfare and Institutions. The experiment is described from the viewpoints of both the welfare department and the School and includes the problems, the plan, and an evaluation.

Kiester, Dorothy J. "Institute Trains Community Action Officials," *Popular Government,* XXXII (October, 1966), 17-19.

Describes the first training series conducted by the Institute of Government of the University of North Carolina for the executive directors of community action agencies established primarily to administer programs funded by the Economic Opportunity Act of 1964.

Lancelot, Yolanda. "Staff Training as an Integrating Factor in Agency Structure," *Public Welfare,* XXII (October, 1964), 263-68.

Using as an example the experience of the Westchester County Division of Family and Child Welfare, the author deals with the closer coordination of services between Child Welfare and Public Assistance.

Lewis, Dena D., and Laing, Ruth. "District Meetings As a Part of In-Service Training in Kansas," *Public Welfare,* V (December, 1947), 277-81.

Description of the planning, content, and evaluation of a series of twelve monthly meetings held at central meeting places over the state for county welfare workers by the Kansas State Division of Public Assistance.

Maginnis, M. Ethel. "Training of New Workers in the Department of Public Welfare of Baltimore City," *Journal of Social Work Process,* X (1959), 12-20.

Variations in the quality of instruction offered by individual supervisors caused the Department to establish a Training Division for new workers in 1951. The training plan focuses on the Public Assistance and Children's Divisions and requires class teaching and supervised practice, and supervision through group conferences rather than individual conferences. Training period is one calendar month, and worker staff is taken on only at the beginning of a training period.

Mayer, Anna B. "Training Child Care Supervisors," *Child Welfare,* XLV (July, 1966), 388-94.

The planning procedures and content of a four year in-service program at Children's Village, Dobbs Ferry, New York, are discussed.

Meyer, Carol H. "A Development Program for Child Welfare Staff," *Children* (July-August, 1961), 141-46.

Since 1958, the New York City Bureau of Child Welfare has been using federal child welfare service's funds for training consultants to devise and administer a demonstration staff program.

National Study Service. *Use of Volunteers in Public Welfare.* New York: New York City Department of Welfare, 1963, 103 pp.

Specific departmental needs and opportunities for volunteers —with job descriptions, qualifications, and training requirements—are included in this study of a suggested program for New York City. Administration of the Program, projected estimates of supervisory staff and training are comprehensively covered. A six-page annotated bibliography is supplied.

Neely, Viola, and Sachs, Virginia. "An In-Service Training Program for Case Aids," *Public Welfare,* III (October, 1945), 225-28.

This article gives the background, description, and training methods of the Central Training Unit of the Cook County

Bureau of Public Welfare in Illinois. It concludes with an outline of the material covered.

Papers Presented on Staff Development Day, Council on Social Work Education Annual Program Meeting, January 22, 1965. Washington, D. C.: United States Welfare Administration, June 16, 1965, 27 pp.

The three papers are: "A Comprehensive Staff Development Program" by Gertrude Leyendecker; "Agency Training Through a National Center" by Arthur Hillman; and "Staff Development for Units of Social Workers in Non-Social Work Organizations" by Addie Thomas. The first paper covers principles, critical points in staff development, and methods. The second talk describes a training center operated by the National Federation of Settlements and Neighborhood Centers at Chicago to supplement local agency in-service training.

Report on a Study of Services, Staffing and Manpower for a Constructive Public Assistance Program in the State of California. New York: Greenleigh Associates, November, 1962, 56 pp.

A survey of county welfare departments in ten of California's largest counties reinforced the view that not nearly enough is being done of a rehabilitative nature, and this is in part due to the lack of training in the social welfare field. "Presently employed personnel must be helped to improve their competence by specially-devised in-service training programs and other staff development measures, including improved administration and supervision, educational leaves and stipends, work-study programs, etc." The report recommends that this training be conducted by the school of social work, but if that is not possible, the State Department of Social Welfare should set up its own "academy" on a decentralized basis.

A Seven-Year Report: The New York State Institute for Public Welfare Training, 1946-1952. Albany: New York State Department of Social Welfare, 1953, 17 pp.

Describes the plan of operation, selection of instructors, content and method of instruction, costs, and evaluation. Appendices include a list of the faculty and various tables of statistics relating to kinds of students, number, and their districts.

Silverblatt, Florence. "A Public Agency Experience in Staff Development," *Journal of Social Work Process,* VII (1956), 17-28.

The program described is one established by the Philadelphia Department of Public Welfare to staff a new program intended to give service to parents of children placed by court action.

Studies in Rehabilitation Counselor Training: Agency-University Communication, Coordination, and Cooperation in Rehabilitation Counselor Education. Minneapolis: Joint Liaison Committee, Council of State Directors of Vocational Rehabilitation and the Rehabilitation Counselor Educators, University of Minnesota, 1964, 44 pp.

Papers presented at a workshop on Rehabilitation Counselor Training planned around the theme of the title.

Training Courses for Cottage Parents in Children's Institutions. New York: Child Welfare League of America, November, 1960, 23 pp.

This publication presents conclusions reached at a meeting sponsored by the League and includes descriptions of fifteen current courses.

Training for Child Care Staff. New York: Child Welfare League of America, 1963, 83 pp.

A compilation of the papers presented at a second conference for those giving and planning training courses for child care staffs in children's institutions. The article also includes a discussion of each paper.

Training for Social Welfare: Proceedings of the Workshop on Staff Training . . . 1964. Ottawa: Committee on Non-Graduate Training, Commission on Education and Personnel, Canadian Welfare Council, October, 1964, 44 pp.

Titles of the most pertinent papers are "In-Service Training and Staff Development"; "Content in Training Programs: Choice, Organization, Evaluation"; "Helps for the Trainer"; and "Training Methods." Includes a four-page selected bibliography.

Training in Public Assistance: A Report Prepared for the Assembly Interim Committee on Social Welfare. Sacramento: California Department of Social Welfare, October, 1958, 19 pp.

A report dealing exclusively with the training of the staffs of county welfare departments engaged in the administration of public assistance; primary focus is on the caseworkers. The report covers the training problem, the way the state department and the county welfare departments are organized to deal with the problem, the nature of current activities in providing on-the-job training, the nature of current activities in using outside training facilities, and suggested directions for the future.

Waldstein, Martha. "A Refresher Course for Married Women Re-Entering the Casework Field," *Social Casework,* XLI (October, 1960), 418-24.

This article describes how and why the course was developed, its students, its content, and evaluations by students and instructors.

"Washington (State) Training of Social Service Supervisors," *Current Practices in Staff Training,* X (June, 1956), 87 pp.

Describes the organization and structure developed for providing training for potential supervisors and includes some of the process used in conducting the sessions as well as considerable material on the content of the sessions.

Weller, Evalyn G., and others. *Building Sound Staff Development.* Chicago: American Public Welfare Association, 1957, 32 pp.

Discusses the staff development function in welfare administration and the purpose and policy of staff training, and describes the staff development program in Kansas.

Wolfrom, Essey. "A Project in Staff Training," *Child Welfare,* XXXVII (November, 1958), 14-17.

The author suggests a program established by Yakima County, with help from the Washington State Department of Public Assistance as one approach to the problem of shortage of trained staff. It is a one-year training program consisting of individual and group conferences. Trainees are public assistance workers transferring to child welfare who usually bring one or more cases with them. The program enables workers without professional training to assume a full caseload in six to nine months, but is not a substitute for professional education.

Willner, Milton. "Values of a Community Training Program for Child-Care Workers," *Social Work,* IV (April, 1959), 94-99.

Presents the views of the workers of the values of a training program as discovered through a survey of the program conducted by the author.

Wyoming: Directors' Guide for Orientation of New Workers. Washington, D. C.: Bureau of Public Assistance, United States Social Security Administration, December, 1957, 55 pp.

Intended for use in counties, the guide sets forth the goals of the agency and the training program, teaching methods, philosophy, and casework techniques, and gives a sample training calendar covering the worker's first four weeks. The guide was prepared originally in the Wyoming Department of Public Welfare and is one in the series, "How They Do It: Illustrations of Practice in the Administration of Public Assistance Programs," published by the Bureau to illustrate current administrative practices in state and other welfare agencies.

Wyoming: Training for County Directors. Washington, D. C.: Bureau of Public Assistance, United States Social Security Administration, 1961, 43 pp.

Presentation of a plan developed by the Wyoming Department of Public Welfare including: (1) the plan for training; (2) the agency in which the plan was developed, the facts that led to its development, and the process by which the development was carried out; and (3) the steps taken to implement it.

2. General References on Purpose, Development, Organization, and Evaluation of Training Programs

Blackey, Eileen A. *Group Leadership in Staff Training.* Washington, D. C.: United States Children's Bureau, 1957, 182 pp.

An effort to apply new knowledge on the functioning of groups to use in educational activities conducted as a part of staff development programs in public welfare agencies. Although the content is primarily addressed to social workers, the problems identified and the framework of concepts used for meeting them are concerns common to all professional groups with educational programs. The publication includes a six-page list of references.

Blum, Arthur. "Innovative Staff Training," *Public Welfare Projected.* Chicago: American Public Welfare Association, 1966, 118-28.

A comprehensive discussion of the problems arising from the shortage of trained personnel, complicated by changing demands on staff resulting from social changes in emphasis in services offered. Suggestions include an institution similar in approach to the police academy, and a special program to sensitize workers to problems of poverty by using Neighborhood Youth Corps youth to accompany students into poverty areas.

California: Guide for Training Analysis. Washington, D. C.: Bureau of Public Assistance, United States Social Security Administration, 1956, 13 pp.

Prepared by the California Department of Social Welfare, this aid for an organized analysis of an on-going training program illustrates recommended practices in the administration of public assistance programs.

Carducci, Dewey J. "A Possible Solution to the Training and Orienting of Child Care Workers," *Child Welfare,* XLI (May, 1962), 212-16.

The author proposes that experienced child care workers be assigned to new "cottage parents" at the beginning of their employment rather than later after incorrect procedures have been developed.

Child Welfare Supervision in Local Public Welfare Agencies. Albany: New York State Department of Social Welfare, August 1, 1956, 84 pp.

All aspects of the supervisor's job are covered in detail in this pamphlet. Section 4, "The Supervisor and the Staff: Supervisory Principles and Methods," deals with the training function, conferences, use of case records, orientation of new workers, and related matters.

Copland, Suzanne. "Training in the Public Welfare Agency," *Public Welfare News,* I (December, 1942), 4-7.

The author elaborates on her position that training for case work includes practical skills, the philosophy of case work, and the practice of combining these in the field.

The Director of Staff Development and Training in Public Welfare. Chicago: Committee on Social Work Education and Personnel, American Public Welfare Association, November 23, 1964, 4 pp.

This is an outline of the scope and responsibilities of the position and the necessary knowledge, skills, abilities, education, and experience required.

Federal Grants for Training of Personnel for Work in the Field of Child Welfare. Washington, D. C.: United States Children's Bureau, 1964, 23 pp.

Gives complete information on how to apply for grants, who is eligible, and how grants should be administered.

Guide for Developing a Friendly Visiting Program. Sacramento: California Department of Social Welfare, 1961, 30 pp.

A guide which recommends training for men, women, and young people to serve as friendly visitors to the aged, disabled, and visually handicapped in nursing homes, homes for the aged, and in their own homes. "Training is essential to the success of the program. The co-sponsor and the welfare department arrange the time, place, content, and speakers based upon the training guide, advice of the community committee and consultants. The trainees will gain the most from sessions which encourage group discussion."

Guide for Training Homemakers. Springfield: Illinois Children and Family Services, 1965, 69 pp.

This course outline includes the history and philosophy of social welfare, personnel policies and procedures, and the various duties of the job.

Hungate, Joseph I. *A Guide for Training Local Public Welfare Administrators.* Washington, D.C.: Divison of Technical Training, Bureau of Family Services, Welfare Administration, Department of Health, Education and Welfare, 1964, 136 pp.

This volume, one of a series of training guides being prepared by the Bureau of Family Services for use of staff development personnel in state and local agencies, discusses the training program, and a series of substantive topics such as administration as a process, the program of the public welfare agency, the philosophical base of welfare programs, federal state relations, job responsibilities, communication in administration, the policy function of administration, and community resources and relationships. Reading assignments, questions for class discussion, method of presenting material, and bibliographies are included.

Mayer, Morris Fritz. "Differential Education and In-Service Training For Child Care Workers," *Child Welfare*, XLIV (May, 1965), 252-61.

"Several categories of child care workers are defined and differential suggestions are made for their training and supervision. Inter- and intra-agency training programs are discussed, and basic content is outlined. A national program for training certified professional child care workers is presented."

Meyer, Carol H. "Staff Development: A Social Work Process in a Public Child Welfare Agency," *Public Welfare*, XX (April, 1962), 125-31.

This article is concerned with the preparation of in-service training programs for staff and focuses on staff development as a function, analysis of goals and purposes, application of concepts of learning, and development of training methods and materials.

Moscrop, Martha. "Augmenting Professional Staff by Means of In-Service Training," *Public Welfare*, X (April, 1952), 34-37, 55.

A discussion of the indispensable, unchanging factors in any staff development program—professional supervision, the written word, and staff evaluation—as well as agency training plans, the selection process, and the training process in staff development programs.

————. *In-Service Training for Social Agency Practice.* Toronto: University of Toronto Press, 1958, 245 pp.

Topics covered in this training manual include: a staff building program, recruiting for in-service training, the extent of the teaching, evaluating the training, and the form of staff development.

Papers Presented on Staff Development Day, Council on Social Work Education Annual Program Meeting, January 22, 1965. Washington, D. C.: United States Welfare Administration, June 16, 1965, 27 pp.

The three papers are: "A Comprehensive Staff Development Program" by Gertrude Leyendecker; "Agency Training Through a National Center" by Arthur Hillman; and "Staff Development for Units of Social Workers in Non-Social Work Organizations" by Addie Thomas. The first paper covers principles, critical points in staff development, and methods. The second talk describes a training center operated by the National Federation of Settlements and Neighborhood Centers at Chicago to supplement local agency in-service training.

Parad, Howard J. "Social Work Training for Child Welfare: Some Key Issues," *Child Welfare*, XL (January, 1961), 1-7.

To provide more effective child welfare service, the author calls for the recruitment and appropriate training of personnel and a new organizational design of services.

A Program of Staff Development. Ottawa: Canadian Welfare Council, 1951, 16 pp.

A report outlining the purpose, organization, and content of a staff development program and suggesting methods for carrying it out.

Report of the Cooperative Project on Public Welfare Staff Training. Washington, D. C.: Division of Technical Training, Bureau of Family Services, United States Department of Health, Education and Welfare, November, 1963.

Covers selected papers and teaching materials presented at the two-week institute and the later return session of one week sponsored by the project. The content of the institute relates to teaching-learning principles and methods in State and local agencies. Volume I covers learning and teaching in public welfare. Volume II covers services to families and children in public welfare.

The Role and Training of Professional Personnel in the Field of Aging. Washington, D. C.: United States White House Conference on Aging, April, 1961, 58 pp.

"A statement of needs, approaches, and programs, together with recommendations." Topics covered include roles for professional personnel, approaches to professional training, and current activity in education and training. The primary emphasis is on university training.

Staff Development in Public Welfare Agencies. Washington, D. C.: United States Bureau of Family Services, 1963, 14 pp.

Although applicable to public welfare agencies at all levels of government, this discussion is most pertinent to larger agencies. For example, the advantages of an orientation center and the function of a separate staff development position are covered. Also included is a three-page discussion of materials and equipment for teaching and learning.

Tannar, Virginia L. *Selected Social Work Concepts for Public Welfare Workers.* Washington, D. C.: United States Bureau of Family Services, 1964, 150 pp.

"This book is intended to be a resource for those who teach public welfare workers. It presents selected basic concepts and principles of social work, and suggests teaching methods designed to help agency workers advance toward the goal of more competent practice." Case studies, lists of supplemental readings, etc. are supplied.

Taylor, Alice L. "Agency Responsibility for Staff Development," *Selected Papers in Group Work and Community Organization Presented at the 79th Annual Meeting, May 25-30, 1952, Chicago, Illinois.* Columbus: National Conference of Social Work, 1953, 91-100.

Specific suggestions concerning content and objectives of staff development programs are based in part on facts from and implications of the Bureau of Labor Statistics survey, "Salaries and Working Conditions of Social Workers in 1950."

————. *The Regional Conference—A Method in Group Consultation: A Report.* Washington, D. C.: Bureau of Public Assistance, United States Social Security Administration, 1950, 70 pp.

A report on a regional conference on staff training which includes a full description of methods used, summaries of discussions, a limited analysis of the group process, and an evaluation of the regional conference as an administrative method.

Training for Social Welfare: Proceedings of the Workshop on Staff Training . . . 1964. Ottawa: Committee on Non-Graduate Training, Commission on Education and Personnel, Canadian Welfare Council, October, 1964, 44 pp.

Titles of the most pertinent papers are "In-Service Training and Staff Development"; "Content in Training Programs: Choice, Organization, Evaluation"; "Helps for the Trainer"; and "Training Methods." Includes a four-page selected bibliography.

The Training of Visiting Homemakers. Ottawa: Canadian Welfare Council, 1963, 8 pp.

This outline of a minimum training course includes reasons for having such a course and how to select trainees as well as the content of the course and how to set it up.

Training Manual for Visitors: Part 1: An Instruction Guide. Springfield: Illinois Public Aid Commission, 1951, 29 pp.

A guide to county superintendents and case work supervisors in the induction of new visitors.

Training Manual for Visitors: Part 2: Skills and Knowledge. Springfield: Illinois Public Aid Commission, 1951, 30 pp.

Part Two is the textbook for Part One. (See above)

Weisbrod, Helen Johnstone. "A Guide for Administrative Planning of Staff Development Responsibilities," *Public Welfare,* XX (July, 1962), 168-69.

A summary of staff development formulation with outlines for the topics of personnel, in-service training, supervision and consultation, and planned educational opportunities.

Weiss, Carol H. "Evaluation of Staff Training Programs," *Welfare in Review,* III (March, 1965), 11-17.

This discussion of evaluation is for use by social agencies, but it contains information applicable to programs of other agencies. Covered are the purposes of evaluation, the relationship between evaluator and trainer, and measures of success.

Weller, Evalyn G. "The Role of a Supervisor of Caseworkers in In-Service Training," *Alabama Social Welfare,* XXVI (January-February, 1961), 17-19.

A discussion of the role of a supervisor of caseworkers in in-service training. Noted are a concept of in-service training; a concept of supervision and the role of the supervisor; the supervisor as an administrator, as a teacher, and enabler; and the in-service training role of the supervisor.

Weller, Evalyn G., and Kilborne, E. B. *Citizen Participation in Public Welfare Programs, Supplementary Services by Volunteers.* Washington, D. C.: Division of Technical Training, Bureau of Public Assistance, United States Social Security Administration, 1956, 46 pp.

Discusses the purpose of supplementary services and offers suggestions for developing volunteer services, and for the orientation, training, and supervision of volunteers. The purpose is to indicate to the staff of state and local welfare agencies it can provide opportunities to citizens to help in extending and improving welfare programs.

Wolfe, Ralph M. Jr. "The Caseworker's Viewpoint of the Role of the Supervisor in In-Service Training," *Public Welfare News,* XXIV (December, 1960), 5-6.

Suggests that emphasis should be placed on individual supervision of new workers. After the worker is established, the emphasis may shift to group training. The article covers in general what the caseworker wants and needs from supervision and training.

Part IV
Bibliographies

Assessment Bibliography. Chicago: International Association of Assessing Officers, 1967, 74 pp.

This bibliography has a section, "Training and Assistance to Assessors," consisting of an annotated list of periodical articles and pamphlets.

"Bibliographical Monography: Education and Training of Public Service Personnel," *International Review of Administrative Sciences,* XXII (1957), 111-17.

International in scope and divided into books, articles, and documents.

Bibliography on Staff Development. Washington, D.C.: Bureau of Public Assistance, United States Social Security Administration, January, 1958, 19 pp.

This bibliography on social welfare training was prepared at the request of the United Nations. Pertinent headings covered are staff development as an aspect of administration, supervision, orientation, group training, consultation, and training of volunteers.

"Executive Development in the Public Service," *Public Personnel Review,* XXI (January, 1960), 77-83.

Prepared by the staff of the United States Civil Service Commission Library, selections in this annotated bibliography were made on the basis of (1) general availability, (2) pertinence to the public service generally, and (3) recentness of material (1953-1959).

Executive Development Methods: Personnel Bibliography. Washington, D. C.: United States Civil Service Commission, 1961, 50 pp.

The fifth in a series of bibliographies on personnel issued by the Library of the United States Civil Service Commission.

Executive Development: Selected References. Washington, D. C.: United States Civil Service Commission, 1954, 8 pp.

A bibliography grouped according to the following subjects: background material, government programs, company programs, evaluation, and development methods.

In-Service Training in Western Europe: A Selected Bibliography. Chicago: Joint Reference Library, 1962, 5 pp.

A bibliography of references pertaining to in-service training in Western Europe.

Management Training in the Public Service: A Selected Bibliography. Chicago: Joint Reference Library, 1963, 2 pp.

Selected references with respect to management training.

Messics, Emil A. *Training in Organizations: Business, Industrial, Government; An Annotated Bibliography on Industrial Training.* Ithaca: New York State School of Industrial and Labor Relations, Cornell University, 1960, 77 pp.

This annotated bibliography of 356 articles, pamphlets, and books, concentrating on the period 1952-60, is divided into the following headings: training-general, employee orientation, work-skill training, technical training and education; supervisory training, management inventory and executive development, group participative learning techniques, audio visual aids, training evaluation, and bibliographies.

Planning, Administration, and Evaluation of Executive Development Programs. Washington, D.C.: United States Civil Service Commission, 1961, 64 pp.

Annotated list covering material on executive development, determination of training needs, program development and administration, and evaluation of training programs.

Planning, Organizing and Evaluating Training Programs: Personnel Bibliography. Washington, D. C.: United States Civil Service Commission, January, 1966, 88 pp.

The primary emphasis in the bibliography is on federal service, but materials are included on other levels of government service, business, and industry.

A Reference List for Firemen's Training. Boston: National Fire Protection Association, 1948, 19 pp.

A selected list of titles prepared to assist instructors and members of firemen's basic or elementary training classes.

A Selected Bibliography for Staff Development. Chicago: American Public Welfare Association, 1946.

A bibliography of books, pamphlets, and articles useful to public welfare agencies in planning for the orientation of new staff, and in planning staff development and in-service training programs.

Selected Bibliography on Supervisory Training. Washington, D. C.: Career Development Program, Bureau of Programs and Standards, Program Planning Division, United States Civil Service Commission, 1956, 12 pp.

The emphasis in this bibliography is on books and articles of practical application.

Service Rating, Training, and Supervision: A Bibliography of Public Personnel Administration Litera- *ture, Part 5.* Washington, D. C.: United States Civil Service Commission, 1949, 172 pp.

The section on training includes, among other topics, specialized training programs and training methods and techniques.

"Supervisory Training," *Public Personnel Review,* XVII (July, 1956), 148-52.

A brief, annotated bibliography of books, pamphlets, and magazine articles on supervisory training prepared by the staff of the United States Civil Service Commission Library.

Index to Bibliography

NOTE: Letters following page numbers indicate the position of items on the page. For example, "b" indicates the second item.

CARL A. RUDISILL LIBRARY
LENOIR RHYNE COLLEGE

Hamann, Albert D., 47d
Hamlin, Clark, 3a
Hands, Glenn, 61f
Hanifin, Frank, 32c
Hankey, Richard O., 45a
Hanna, R. E., 32d
Hardy, William R., 12f, 13L, 13m, 16m
Harrell, C. A., 13n
Harrington, U. J., 29b
Harrison, Leonard H., 53f
Hartman, Earl P., 54c
Harvard University, 16h
Haug, Dean Russell, 20d
Havlick, J. Robert, 56i
Hayworth, Thadene, 58a
Hediburg, R., 34f
Heisel, W. D., 13n
Herman, Allen B., Jr., 45b
Hess, Fred, 45c
Higher Education Act of 1965, 1a
Hilliker, Floyd, 32e, 45d
Hillman, Arthur, 64a, 66e
Hinds, George L., 13o
Hoag, James F., 59i
Hobart, James C., 13p
Hofheinz, Roy, 36L
Holcomb, R. L., 49e, 52k
Holl, W. K., 54c
Hollinger, Lindon S., 13q, 20e
Hollingsworth, Dan, 53g
Holmgren, R. Bruce, 45e, 51d
Holster, William, 45f
Honey, John C., 16a
Honolulu, Hawaii. Department of Civil Service, 5h, 59h
Hookey, Edward M., 8g
Hoover, John Edgar, 45g, 57b
Housing Act of 1964, 5e, 40e
Houston, Texas, 36L
Howard, John P., 51e
Howard, S. Kenneth, 11e
Hudiburg, Everett, 35a
Hughes Aircraft Company. Education and Training Research Laboratories, 32b, 34n
Humphrey, Jackson C., 63e
Hungate, Joseph I., 65m
Hunger, John M., 58b
Hunter, Donald F., 40h
Huntley, Robert J., 58c
Huttner, Ludwig, 17m

I

Illinois, 45m
    Children and Family Services, 65L
    Department of Public Welfare, 63b
    Public Aid Commission, 63c, 67b, 67c
    University. Institute of Government and Public Affairs, 21g, 28d
        Library School, 39j
        School of Social Work, 62f, 63a
Indiana. Board of Tax Commissioners, 28a
    University, 16h, 60i
Ingram, William T., 61g
Institute for Local Self Government, Berkeley, 14i
Institute of Public Administration, New York, 18b
Institute of Public Administration, Toronto, 17g
Insurance Institute for Highway Safety, 57d
International Association of Assessing Officers, 26L, 26m, 26n, 27i, 28h, 69a
International Association of Chiefs of Police, 43b, 43g, 46m, 47c, 48b, 50j, 50L, 51j, 52k, 52n, 53e, 55k, 57L

International Association of Fire Chiefs, 33h, 33i, 33k
International City Managers' Association, 1e, 1g, 1h, 4d, 4e, 5i, 6a, 6e, 6g, 7n, 13c, 13e, 13j, 14a, 14j, 15a, 15e, 15g, 15j, 16d, 16f, 16o, 17h, 18j, 19c, 19g, 19L, 28o, 29g, 32k, 39d, 41a, 46j, 52a, 57g, 59k, 60h, 60o
    Advanced Management Training Program, 15h
    Institute for Training in Municipal Administration, 12L, 19L, 32n, 35h
    Joint Management Program Committee, 15f
    Twin Cities Chapter, Minneapolis, 13b
International Conference of Building Officials, 40c
Iowa, 59i
    Development Commission, 40j
    State University, Fire Service Extension, 34h
    Institute of Public Affairs, 11b
Irivendale, California, 2g
Ittner, Ruth, 3c
Ives, Jane K., 24j, 26b, 26c

J

Jackson, Michigan, 13g, 58i
Jacobs, David L. G., 57c
Jacobsen, Adolph, 32g
Jameson, Samuel Haig, 51g
Jelf, R. W., 45j
Jenkins, Bette, 40k
Jenkins, Wilbur L., 20h
Jensen, D. A., 63g
Johnson, B. W., 18c
Johnson, Martin W., 45k, 51h
Johnson, William A., 45L
Johnson City, New York, 61k
Joint Commission on Correctional Manpower and Training, Washington, D.C., 23b
Joint Reference Library, Chicago, 69g, 69h
Just, J. W., 32h
Juvenile Delinquency and Youth Offenses Control Act, 24a, 24L, 25g

K

Kansas, 49a, 64L
    State Division of Public Assistance, 63j
    University. Bureau of Governmental Research, 50g
        Governmental Research Center, 3e, 12m, 14k, 15k, 17j, 30e, 30g, 31a, 38k, 47f, 56j
Kansas City, Missouri, 16j, 21L, 30c, 54j
    Police Department, 45h
Kassaoff, Norman C., 45m
Kennedy, John P., 55d
Kentucky, 28g
    Department of Child Welfare, 62m
Keuper, Vincent P., 45n
Kiester, Dorothy J., 63h
Kilborne, E. B., 67g
Kilpatrick, Wylie, 29d
Kimball, Warren Y., 34d
Kimble, Joseph P., 51i
King, S. D. M., 6m
Kirkpatrick, Donald L., 6n
Klein, Charles T., 8i
Klein, Robert N., 59j
Kline, James S., 56j
Klinger, T. S., 3d
Kopec, Chester J., 7j
Korb, L. David, 17n, 17o
Kreml, Franklin M., 51j, 51k

L

La Habra, California. Fire Department, 33o, 35o
    Police Department, 50a

Morris, Theodore P., 14f, 19h
Morris, Willard B., 46h
Moscrop, Martha, 66c, 66d
Moseley, H. M., 51n
Mosher, Frederick C., 18e
Muehleisen, Gene S., 46i, 47c
Mueniter, Otis, 35g
Muhlbach, George W., 53h
Municipal League of New Mexico, 28k, 30f
Municipal Manpower Commission, 2d, 3L
Murphy, Patrick V., 46l, 46m
Murray, William G., 27h

N

Nash, Peter H., 41b
Nassau County, New York, 33e
National Association of Assessing Officers, 27e
National Association of Housing Officials, 40g, 42b
National Association of Housing and Redevelopment Officials, 40n, 41h
National Association of Local Government Officers, London, 4c
National Association of Real Estate Boards, 40i
National Civil Service League, 20g, 21j
National Conference of Social Work, 66L
National Federation of Settlements and Neighborhood Centers, Chicago, 64a, 66e
National Fire Protection Association, Boston, 33n, 34d, 35m, 35n, 69L
National Housing Act of 1964, 27g
National Institute of Public Affairs, 5d, 12j, 16h, 18e
National League of Cities, 42g
National Municipal Review, 12k, 20b, 57h
National Planning Conference, San Francisco, 1957, 41c
National Probation and Parole Association Journal, 25i
National Research Council. Highway Research Board, 59d
National Safety Council, 57f
National Study Service, 63n
Nebraska. University, 54a
Neely, Viola, 63o
Neighborhood Youth Corps, 65d
Neosho, Missouri, 61f
New Canaan, Connecticut, 14b
New Hampshire. University. Department of Government, 11e
New Jersey, 48e, 62n
    Division of Mental Retardation, 39h
    Division of Taxation, 28f
    Housing Authority, 41k
    Law Enforcement Council, 46c
    Police Training Commission, 43m
New Mexico. Highway Department, 59p
New Orleans, Louisiana. Housing Authority, 40a
New South, 56e
New York (State), 36c, 38f, 46b, 49j, 50e
    Board of Equalization and Assessment, 26h
    Bureau of Fire Mobilization and Control, 35b, 35c
    Department of Audit and Control, 29i, 29j, 30m
    Department of Civil Service, 37c
    Department of Conservation, 61a
    Department of Health, 36d, 61g
    Department of Social Welfare, 64c, 65g
    Division of Safety, 34q
    Institute for Public Welfare Training, 64c
    Interdepartmental Health and Hospital Council, 37c
    Office for Local Government. Division of Fire Safety, 31e, 33a, 35f, 35i
        Municipal Police Training Council, 45i, 46k, 51f, 53j
    School of Industrial and Labor Relations of Cornell University, 69i
    School for Police, 46e

University College at New Paltz, 37c
New York (City), 5a, 5m, 15i, 32h
    Bureau of Child Welfare, 63m
    Bureau of Public Health Education, 37k
    Bureau of the Budget, 16g
    Chamber of Commerce, 20L
    City College. Baruch School. Joint Police Science Program, 44n, 46f
    Civil Service Commission, 2i
    Department of Correction, 24m
    Department of Health, 36g
    Department of Personnel, 14c
    Department of Welfare, 63f, 63n
    Fire Department, 32m
    Housing Authority Police Force, 41i, 48i
    Intern Program, 39g
    Office of the Mayor, 32h
    Police Academy, 44i, 44j, 44n, 56d
    Police Department, 43e, 46f, 46L, 47k, 53n
    Youth Board, 23f
New York State Association of City and Village Clerks, 29j, 30m
New York State Society of Municipal Finance Officers, 29j, 30m
New York University. Graduate School of Public Administration and Social Service, 13h, 14c
Newark, New Jersey, 13i
Newark, Ohio, 44b
Newman, Charles L., 26i
Newton-Wellesley Hospital, 37g
Neyhart, Amos E., 46n
Nielsen, Judith, 47a
Nigro, Felix, 7b
Nimmo, George M., 47b
Noble, Henry J., 24m
Noffsinger, Forest R., 57e
Nolting, Orin F., 4d, 14j, 32n
Norfolk, Virginia, 58i
North Carolina, 37d, 48j
    State Highway Patrol Schools, 57a
    University. Institute of Governments, 2h, 5b, 5k, 12h, 15L, 42h, 63h
        School of Social Work, 62k, 62L
Northwestern University. Department of Political Science, 8d
    Traffic Institute, 44f, 45k, 51h, 52L, 56L, 56m, 57c, 57e, 57i, 57m
Northwest Iowa Mayors' Association, 11c
Norwood, Ohio, 44h
Nova Scotia, Canada, 29b
Nowak, Edward J., 29h

O

Oakes, James W., 7c
Oakland, California, 9a
Oakland University. Office of Continuing Education, 13d
O'Brien, Donald M., 32o
O'Brien, Henry, 37d
O'Brien, Joseph F., 38f
Ocheltree, Keith, 54d
O'Connor, George W., 47c
Odiorne, George S., 18f
Ohio, 49a
    Law Enforcement Officer Training Program, 50b
    Peace Officers Training Council, 47e, 47j
    State University. Bureau of Educational Research, 60e
        Library, 21k, 39L
Oklahoma. Department of Health, 37i
    State University. Department of Fire Protection Technology, 35a, 35e, 35L

College of Business, 14L
Oklahoma University, 34f
O'Leary, Vincent A., 25a
Olmstead, Donald W., 54m
Olsen, Allan S., 4e, 18g
Olsen, Leif O., 19m
Oram, Phyllis G., 37g
Oregon, 49k
    Board of Higher Education, 16e
    State Tax Commission, 26e, 27d
    State University, 26e
O'Reiley, Patrick, 54e
Owens, Robert G., 47d

P

Pacific Coast Building Officials Conference, 40i
Parad, Howard J., 66f
Parker, Beulah, 39a
Parker, R. S., 18h
Parnicky, Joseph J., 39h
Pasadena, California, 14f, 54c
    City College, 31j
    Personnel Department, 19h, 20n
Patteson, Samuel A., Jr., 27i
Pennsylvania, 45m, 49a, 61d
    Board of Parole, 24b, 24c
    Department of Internal Affairs, 12d, 30o
    Field Training Center, Pittsburgh, 37a
    Municipal Police Officers' Standards and Training Commission, 42k
    Public Service Institute, 24k, 31c
    State Bureau of Youth Services, 55j
    State Department of Public Instruction, 5L, 24k
    State Police Academy, Hershey, 56h
Pennsylvania Chiefs of Police Association, 24b, 26j, 42k, 44d, 48m, 50d, 55h, 55i, 56h
Peoria, Illinois, 52i
Peper, John P., 42l, 47g, 47h, 53i
Perreault, John O., 4f
Personnel, 8a, 9b, 17m, 17n, 18d
Personnel Administration, 2k, 5j, 6b, 6n, 6p, 7d, 7f, 8L, 13m, 16c, 17f, 19d, 19j, 57o
Personnel Journal, 16p, 19m
Peterson, D. R., 36n
Petrie, Harry P., 41c
Philadelphia, Pennsylvania, 55j, 55m
    Department of Public Welfare, 64d
Phillips, Charles W., 37f
Phoenix, Arizona, 1d, 21h
    Fire Department, 34i
Pierce, Donald M., 62b
Pietrus, Joseph T., 9b
Pittsburgh, Pennsylvania, 55j
    Fire Department, 31b
    Housing Authority, 40o
    University. Graduate Center for Public Works, 59c
        Graduate School of Public International Affairs, 41d
        Institute of Local Government, 11g
Pittsburgh Plate Glass Foundation, 41d, 41e
Police Training Act of New Jersey, 43j
Pomrenke, Norman E., 52b
Port of New York Authority. Police Academy, 47i
Portland. Fire Department, 35j
Porter, Lyman W., 18d
Powers, Stanley, 21a
Price, Kendall O., 7d
Princeton University, 16h
Prior, Margaret M., 37n
Public Administration News, 20a

Public Administration Service, 43f, 50k
Public Management, 1e, 2d, 3k, 4e, 4m, 4n, 5b, 5k, 5n, 6e, 8h, 11d, 12L, 12n, 13a, 13c, 13g, 13n, 13p, 14a, 15c, 15h, 15L, 16j, 16k, 18c, 18g, 20i, 20k, 21a, 21b, 43i, 48o
Public Personnel Association, 7j, 8c, 8j, 18b, 54d
Public Personnel Review, 1f, 2e, 4i, 5f, 5m, 6c, 6d, 6j, 8i, 9a, 14f, 16b, 20h, 52o, 53p, 54b, 57c, 58a, 59o, 69d, 70c
Pueblo, Colorado, 49a
Purcell, P., 52n
Purdy, E. Wilson, 52d
Purnell, Robert L., 26n, 27i
Pursuit, Dan G., 25b, 55g

R

Rafferty, Max, 35k
Ralston, Lee W., 48c
Reese, Howard L., 21h
Reilly, Donald F., 59o
Reining, Henry, Jr., 4i
Reock, Ernest C., Jr., 4j, 26m
Richman, Grover C., Jr., 48e
Richmond, Maurice S., 62b
Richmond, Virginia, 4f
Ridley, Clarence E., 1e, 15c
Ritvo, Miriam M., 37g
Riverside, California. Peace Officers' Training Center, 47g
Rizos, E. John, 21b
Roberts, C. A., 48f
Robinson, R. L., 4L
Rochester, New York. Police Bureau, 48g, 52e
Roebuck, Julian, 25d
Rogers, Howard L., 52f, 52g
Rogers, J. S., 49e, 52k
Rogers, James C., 33e
Romani, John H., 4m
Romilly, Edgar P., 61h, 61i
Rose, J. T., 26n
Rosenberger, Homer T., 7e
Rosenthal, Eleanor, 15d
Royal Institute of Public Administration, 17c
Russell, Bernard, 25e, 25f
Russell, C. W., 48h
Rutgers University. Bureau of Government Research, 4j, 27j, 30n
Ryan, John W., 54n

S

Sachs, Virginia, 63o
Sacramento County, California. Probation Department, 23e
Saginaw, Michigan, 3k, 14e
Saint Joseph, Missouri, 63e
Saint Joseph County, Indiana, 38g
Saint Louis, Missouri, 2o
    Police Department, 50j
    University, 62g
        School of Social Service. Institute for Delinquency Control, 24h
Saint Petersburg, Florida, 13c
San Antonio, Texas. Housing Authority, 40i
San Bernardino Valley College, 33m
San Diego, California, 29f, 54b, 54e
    Director of Public Works, 59f
San Diego County, California. Department of Civil Service and Personnel Training Division, 3g
San Francisco, California. Chief of Police, 55n
San Joaquin, California. Mosquito Abatement District, 38a
Sanderson, B. M., 59p
Santa Ana, California. Police Department, 42d
Sarvis, Robert G., 60a

Savannah, Georgia. Civil Service Commission, 3d
   Vocational School, 3d
Savings and Loan League, 40i
Schaefer, Norman C., 37i
Schatz, Donald, 41i, 48i
Scheidt, Edward, 48j
Schlesinger, Lawrence, 7f
Schrader, George R., 7g, 15e
Schriever, Paul, 4n
Schroeder, Oliver, Jr., 48k
Schrotel, Stanley R., 57j
Schten, Edward V., 58b
Schultz, Douglas G., 52h
Schwab, Eleanor, 1h
Schwer, Arthur E., Jr., 62c
Scott, C. L., 33g
Scruggs, B. L., 30d
Seale, Edwin L., 48ʟ
Seares, Robert S., 54j
Sears Roebuck Foundation .City Planning Fellowship Program,
   40d
Seattle-King County Department of Health, 36n
Seckler-Hudson, Catheryn, 7h
Shaffer, Paul E., 41c
Shank, Russell, 39f
Shannon, Francis John, 28g
Sharpe, Carleton F., 15h
Shaw, Kennedy, 7i
Sheil, Marion D., 21c, 39i
Sherwood, Frank P., 4i, 18j
Shurtleff, James F., 41b
Siegel, Arthur I., 52h
Sills, Arthur J., 48n
Silverblatt, Florence, 64d
Silvern, Leonard C., 32b, 33j, 34n
Silverstone, David M., 53k
Skillman, George C., 29n
Smalley, A. T., 52n
Smigielski, W. K., 41m
Smith, Julian W., 61j
Smith, Norman R., 7j
Snibbe, Richard H., 48p
Society for Personnel Administration, 7e, 8b, 18ʟ, 19b, 18e
Society for the Advancement of Management, 16ʟ
Solem, Allen R., 8ʟ, 19j
Soller, Genevieve R., 37i, 37j
Sommers, William A., 52i
Sopp, George C., 62h
Sorensen, Clyde A., 54k
Soule, Rolland L., 53l, 53m
South Carolina. University. Bureau of Public Administration,
   2f, 5c
   Law Enforcement Training School, 45b
South Carolina Educational Television Center, 47a
South Dakota, 27i
   University. Governmental Research Bureau, 26f, 28e
Southern California. Joint College-Federal Service Council, 20c
   University, 44g
      Delinquency Control Institute, 25b, 55g
      Institute of Public Administration, 12n
      School of Public Administration, 4i, 20d
      Youth Studies Center, 55d
Southern Methodist University. Institute of Management, 15e
Southern Regional Education Board, 41ʟ
Spiegel, Allen D., 37i
Springfield, Missouri, 57i
Stahl, O. Glenn, 7ʟ
Stallmann, Esther L., 39j
Stanford University, 16h

Stanley, David T., 5a, 15i
State Government, 7k, 21j, 25a, 41n, 46d, 46h, 49ʟ, 50e
Stene, Edwin O., 15j
Stewart, Alva, W., 5b, 15ʟ
Stewart, Ward, 16a
Stone, Donald D., 60c
Stoner, John E., 60i
Stottler, Richard H., 49e, 52k
Stoudemire, Robert H., 5c
Stover, Carl F., 5d
Studt, Elliot, 25f
Sulkin, Howard A., 8k
Sullivan, John W., 18k
Swab, Robert D., Jr., 25h, 26j, 55h, 55i, 55j
Sweeney, Faye B., 49f

T
Tandy, William J., 16b
Tannar, Virginia L., 66k
Taylor, Alice L., 66ʟ
Taylor, Bill N., 16c
Taylor, Edward M., 26k
Temby, L. E., 33m
Tennessee, 28ʟ, 60f
   Board of Vocational Education, 33c
   State Planning Commission, 40ʟ
Texas. Division of Defense and Disaster Relief, 34c, 35g
   Firemen's Training School, 34j
   University, 29ʟ
Texas Municipal League, Austin, 12b
Thomas, Addie, 64a, 66e
Thompson, Herbert W., 21g
Thomson, Louis M., Jr., 49g
Thriscutt, Herbert Sydney, 57k
Toledo. Police Academy, 49g
Town and County Officers Training School of the State of New
   York, 31g, 33f, 60b
Town Planning Institute. North of England Division, 41m
Trimmer, Albert J., 52ʟ, 57m
Trezise, Fred W., 60k
Tucson, Arizona, 13p
   Department of Administration. Budget and Research Divi-
   sion, 20j
Tulane University. School of Social Work, 25k

U
Underwood, Bruce, 37m
United States. Agency for International Development, 30k
   Bureau of Employment Security, 8g
   Bureau of Family Services, 65m, 66h, 66j, 66k
   Bureau of Labor Statistics, 66ʟ
   Bureau of Public Assistance, 6f, 65a, 65b, 65e, 66m, 67g, 69c
   Children's Bureau, 23a, 24f, 24g, 25f, 25j, 55c, 65c, 65j
   Civil Service Commission, 5g, 8n, 17e, 17o, 69d, 69e, 69f,
   69k, 70a, 70b, 70c
   Congress. House of Representatives, 48b
   Department of Health, Education and Welfare, 19k, 24e, 37e
   Department of Labor, 17ʟ
   Housing and Home Finance Agency, 33i, 39g, 40e, 42a
   Library of Congress. Legislative Reference Service, 2ʟ
   National Institute of Health, 36k
   National Security Agency, 18a
   Office of Education, 13g, 16a
   Office of Juvenile Delinquency and Youth Development, 24a,
   25g
   President's Committee on Juvenile Delinquency and Youth
   Crime, 24ʟ
   President's Commission on Law Enforcement and Adminis-
   tration of Justice, 47n, 47o

78

Public Health Service, 36f, 36m, 37d, 37i, 37j, 37L, 38c, 38d, 38g, 38h
Public Housing Administration, 40n, 41j
Social Security Administration, 8e, 8f, 8m, 16n
Surgeon General's Air Pollution Committee, 37p
Urban Renewal Administration, 41h
Veterans Administration, 18m
Welfare Administration, 24a, 64a, 66e
White House Conference on Aging, 37h, 66i
University City, Missouri, 2o
University of Notre Dame, 5k
Urie, John M., 21h
Urquhart, Raymond M., 49j
Utah. State Board for Vocational Education, 35d

V

Van Asselt, Karl A., 49k, 49L
Van Buren, James K., 37n
Vanderburg, D. Robert, 16i
Van Heuvelen, W., 62j
Vermont. University. Government Research Center, 12g
Vickers, S. E., 21i
Virginia, 26n, 27i, 37d, 62e
　Department of Health, 38b
　　University, 16h
　　　Bureau of Public Administration, 27m
　　　Institute of Government, 27b
Virginia Association of Assessing Officers, 27b
Virginia Homemakers Service of Northeastern Nevada, 36m

W

Waggoner, Hugh H., 49m
Wagner, Donald C., 20a
Waldstein, Martha, 64j
Walker, H. Thomas, 39k
Walker, Robert N., 55k
Wall, John, 25k
Warner, Kenneth O., 30a
Washington Court House, Ohio, 47L
Washington, D.C. Military District, 48L
Washington (State), 64k
　Board for Vocational Education, 32a, 34m
　Department of Public Assistance, 64m
　Legislature. Joint Committee on Governmental Cooperation, 49n
　University. Division of Governmental Studies and Service, 12a
Washington Association of County Commissioners, Olympia, 12a
Washington University, 62g
Water Pollution Control Federation, 62b, 62c
Watson, James R., 21j
Watson, Nelson A., 55k
Watt, Graham W., 16j
Wayne State University. Department of Political Science. Government Research and Service Staff, 13o
Wayne Township, New Jersey, 38h
Weaver, Fred D., 9a
Weber, Charles S., 7k, 41n

Weisbrod, Helen Johnstone, 67d
Weiss, Carol H., 67e
Weiss, Robert L., 37o
Weller, Evalyn G., 64L, 67f, 67g
West Virginia, 32d, 37d
　University. Department of Mining and Industrial Extension, 32q
Westchester County. Division of Family and Child Welfare, 63i
Western Actuarial Bureau, 31L
Western City, 1d, 2g, 21h, 58j
Western Interstate Commission for Higher Education, 24i
Western Reserve University. Law-Medicine Center, 48k
Westmeyer, Troy R., 5j
Weston, Conley W., 38i
Whale, Malcolm D., 34a, 36b
Whisenand, Paul M., 49o, 52m
White, Larry C., 58j
Whitesell, William E., 9b
Whittier, California, 53o
Wichita, Kansas. Fire Department, 33p, 35p
　Police Department, 47p
　University. Center for Urban Studies, 47p, 54i
Wilcox, Robert F., 30b
Willis, Charles A., 8h
Willner, Milton, 64n
Wilson, Celianna I., 21k, 39L
Wilson, H. L., 50a
Winfrey, Robley, 60L
Winger, Robert M., 34b, 36i
Winkler, Frank J., 50b
Winston, Oliver C., 42i
Wisconsin. Department of Taxation, 28b
　University. Bureau of Government, 23g, 54n, 58b
　　Engineering Experiment Station, 61n, 62a
Wolfe, Ralph M., Jr., 67h
Wolfer, D. P., 16k
Wolfrom, Essey, 64m
Wolke, Michael S., 25L, 55L
Wood, Alan C., 50c
Woodford, Dorothy, 21L, 30c
Woodson, C. W., Jr., 52n
Worcester, Massachusetts. Personnel Department, 16L
Wunsch, Edward F., 50d
Wyoming. Department of Public Welfare, 65a, 65b
　Law Enforcement Academy, 47b
　University. Division of Adult Education and Community Service, 29k

Y

Yakima County, Washington, 64m
York, Orrell A., 50e

Z

Zanner, Theodore, 5m
Zelhart, Paul, 25d
Ziegler, Richard C., 39h
Zimmerman, John, 17m
Zimmerman, Joseph F., 12k, 16L, 42j